CABO BOB'S
MEXICAN HUMOR 201

Authored By Cabo Bob, Who Also Brought You MEXICAN SLANG 101

Published in USA
by Adoro Books
In Mexico by
AdoroLibros, SA

THE PURPOSE OF THIS BOOK

This book was created to serve several purposes. The most obvious is as collection of jokes and other humor. Secondly, it's an aid to students of Spanish. Jokes, like songs, stick in the memory and can help with speech patterns as well as vocabulary. I've tried to introduce interesting words and locutions in the stories. Beyond that, learning jokes and sayings like this does much to ease the transition into another country or culture. There is little new here: these are more "classics" and everyday speech patterns. But dropping them to neighbors, bar companions, or business principals can lead to learning more, to being a more "regular fellow", and the usual social lubricant of laughter.

Fans of our "Mexican Slang 101" often remark that it helps assimilation... and to picking up more of "normal" Mexican Spanish, and we'd like to think that "Spanish Humor 201" can also serve as an adjunct to your studies. In addition to serving as "bathroom reading", and just a collection of great jokes that non-Spanish-speakers might not be familiar with.

CONTENTS   CONTENIDO

Top Ten Jokes	Sala De La Fama	2
Men	Hombres	21
Women	Mujeres	25
For Kids	Por Niños	30
Nuns	Monjas	33
Priests	Padres	40
Marriage	Matrimonio	43
Mothers In Law	Suegras	47
Cheating	Sanchos	49
Doctors	Medicos	55
Waiters	Meseros	65
Dummies	Estupidos	70
Drunks	Borrachos	78
Border Jokes	Fronterizos	81
Bilingual Jokes	Bilingues	86
Christmas Jokes	Navideños	93
Quickies	Rapidines	99
International	Mundial	101
Miscellaneous	Varios	117
Sayings	Dichos	167
Pronunciation	Pronuciar	176
About Cabo Bob	El Autor	179
More Cool Books	Mas Libros	180

1. LLAMAME

Se encuentran en la calle dos amigas que no se veian desde hace mucho tiempo:

- Hola ¿cómo estás? le dice una.
- Bien, ¿y tú qué has hecha? le dice la otra.
- Ya me gradué de la escuela.
- Ah! yo también!
- Ya me casé.
- Ah! yo también!
- Ya tuve un bebé.
- Ah! yo también!
- Tengo que irme amiga... cuídate mucho

- Llámame.
- ¡Yo también!

CALL ME

Two girlfriends who haven't seen each other in a long time meet in the street.

- Hey, how are you? the first woman asks.

- Good, and you? What have been doing?" says the other woman.

- Well, I graduated from school.

- Ah, me, too!

- I got married.

- Ah, me, too!

- And I have a baby now.

- Ah, me, too!

- I have to go, girlfriend… take care.

- Call me.

-Ah, me, too!

Works on the pun between **llámame** –call me—and **ya mamé**—I already sucked (I gave head).

2. TRATAMIENTO

Despues de casarse con un ruquin ricardo, la sexisima chava regresa de la luna de miel y todas las amigas la reciben con una fiesta.

Dice ella, "¡Qué emoción, gracias manitas!", pero ellas inmediamente preguntan, "Rapido, dinos ¿Qué tal te fue?"

"¡Uy, de pelicula!" contesta, "Fuimos a un crucero por el caribe y conocí paradisíacas islas. Fuimos a Nueva York donde me llenó de joyas y ropa cara!"

Pero gritan las amigas, "¡Eso no nos importa! Queremos saber, ¿Como te fue en el sexo?"

"Ah, en lo sexual," dice sonriendo la muchacha, "Bueno, como ya está un poco viejo, estamos en tratamiento."

"¿Eh?" y "¿Ah, si?" dicen la amigas, "¿Como está eso?"

"Simple," contesta la recien casada, "Mientras él trata, yo miento."

THE TREATMENT

After getting married to a "golden oldie", the sexy chick returns from her honeymoon and all her friends throw her a party.

She says, "How wonderful, thanks girls," but they immediately ask, "Quick, tell us, how was it?"

"Oh, like a movie," she answers, "We went on a cruise ship to the Caribbean and I saw some island paradises. Then we went to New York, where he covered me with jewels and expensive clothes."

But her pals yell, "We don't care about that! We want to know how was the sex?"

"Ah, the sexual aspects, " says the girl, smiling, "Well, since he's a little old, we're in treatment."

"Oh?" and "What?" say her friends, "What's that all about?"

"Simple," says the newlywed, "He tries, I lie."

Works on the the play on **trata** (try) and **miento** (I lie). **Ruquín** is a form of **ruco**, meaning "old". **Ricardo** means "rich" or a rich man.

3. TECOLOTE

(Mejor actuado que puro hablado)

Un pareja de inditos fueron a la feria de su pueblo. Al llegar se dirigieron al juego de reventar los globos, en el cual ganaron derecho a un animal de peluche, entonces el indito le preguntó a su esposa, "Vieja que queres?"

La indita dijo, "El tuculote viejo." (tecolote).

Al llegar a su jacal se encontraron con su compadre y el indito gritó, "Veja, vieja ven!"

Su esposa dijo: "Que queres viejo?"

"Enséñale el tuculote a mi compadre."

La indita hizo vuelta, se subio la falda, se bajó los calzones y le enseñó las nalgas.

El indito gritó, "Vieja pindija, el de peluche, el de peluche."

La indita se subio la falda, se bajó los calzones y le muestra el chapulín colorado.

THE OWL

(Better acted out than just told)

A pair of Indian hicks went to the carnival in their town. Once there, they ended up at a balloon-popping game, where he won his choice of plush animals and asked his wife, "Honey, what do you want?"

She said, "The owl, honey."

Getting back to their hut, they met a friend and the guy yelled, "Woman, come here."

His wife said, "Want do you want?"

"Show your owl to my compadre."

She turned around, raised her skirt, lowered her panties and showed him her ass.

Her husband yelled, "Supid woman, the fuzzy one, the fuzzy one!"

So she raised her skirt, lowered her panties and showed her pussy.

Note the "hick" pronunciations of some of these words, including the big pun here: **tecolote** which gets confused with **tu culote**, an augmentative of culo, which is used for both "ass" and "pussy".

Peluche means "plush", thus any stuffed toy like an **oso de peluche**, referring to a Teddy bear or anything fuzzy or fleecy.

Also note **chapulín colorado** -- red grasshopper--for "pussy".

4. CONTRATADO

Un dia San Pedro estaba haciendo su trabajo rutinario a las puertas del cielo, cuando notó que una de ellas se habia colgado, por que necesitaba una rápida reparación. Salió y se dirigió a la fila de personas que esperaban su turno para entrar. "¿Hay aquí algún herrero?"

Tres hombres levantaron la mano: un africano, un italiano, y un mexicano. San Pedro les pidió que revisaron la puerta y le hicieran un presupuesto.

El africano se acercó la puerta, la revisó, y estimó que con $900 dolares quedaria arreglado el trabajo. Calculó $300 para materiales, $300 para la mano de obra, y $300 para el.

El siguiente fue el italiano, el cual revisó a conciencia cada parte de la puerta: "Estas son las puertas más hermosas que haya visto. Casi podria decirse que fueron hechas in italia, de hecho en Florencia, durante el Renacimiento. Una verdadera abra maestra. El costo par arreglas la puerta será de tres mill dollares: mil para los materiales, mil para la fina mano de obra italiana, y mil para mi."

San Pedro da las gracias y pide el presupuesto al mexicano. Este dio un rápido vistazo a la puerta y le dice a San Pedro: "Serian $2900 dolares. Mil para ti, mil para mi...y contratamos al africano."

HIRED

One day St. Peter was doing his routine work on the doors of heaven, when he noticed that one of them had hung up and needed quick repair. He went out and spoke to the line of people waiting their turn to get in: "Is there a smith here?"

Three men raised their hands, an African, an Italian, and a Mexican. St. Pete asked them to inspect the door and make an estimate.

The African approached the door, inspected it, and estimated he could do it for $900. He broke it down to $300 for materials, $300 for labor, and $300 for himself.

Next was the Italian, who conscientiously inspected every part of the door. "These are the most beautiful doors I've ever seen. I can almost tell you that they were made in Italy, in Florence in fact, during the Renaissance. A true masterpiece. The cost to fix the door will be $3000. A thousand for materials, a thousand for fine Italian labor, and a thousand for me."

St. Peter thanked him and asked the Mexican for an estimate. He gave the door a quick glance and said to St. Peter, "It'll be $2900. A thousand for you, a thousand for me...and we'll hire the African."

5. SUEGRAZO

Un joven campesino disfrutó las delicias de dos sabrosisimas chavas con el truco viejo de prometir a las dos que se casaria despues. Esta decepcion resulto tremendo por el muchacho, pero tambien tuvo resultados menos alegres: dos embarazos en el mismo pueblito, y con el mismo progenitor.

Al saber de la condicion de sus hijas, las dos mamas armaran birinches con el joven, pero aun mas una con otra cuando se dieron cuenta que fueron dos novias y solamente un novio. Total que el caso se llevo ante el juez de paz, quien reconocia inmediamente que necesito la sabiadura del Rey Salomon.

Entonces dijo el juez que la solucion fuera partir al acusado en dos, y darle una parte a cada quejosa. Una de las mamas grito, "Ay no! Pobre muchacho. Como le van a hacer semejante cosa?

Pero la otra mama dijo, "Eso! Eso! Que lo partan. Mas, que lo descuarten!"

Y mirando a la segunda madre, el juez sentencia: "El chico se casa con su hija! Usted es la veradera suegra!"

MOTHER IN LAW DEAREST

A young farmer enjoyed the delights of two extremely tasty girls through the old trick of promising to marry them afterwards. This deception turned out great for the guy, but had less happy results for the girls: two pregnancies in the same town, with the same perpetrator.

Upon finding out about the condition of their daughters, the two mothers had two separate tantrums with the young man, but as soon as they became aware of the other girl and mama they really flipped out. So much so that the case was brought before the Justice of the Peace, who immediately recognized a case that would call for the wisdom of Solomon.

So he said that the solution would be to cut the alleged future father in two, and give one piece to each complainant.

One of the mothers cried, "Oh no, the poor boy! How could you do such a thing?"

But the other mother said, "That's it! That's it! Cut him in two. Better yet, cut him in quarters!"

So with Solomon's wisdom, the judge looked at the second mother and passed sentence: "The boy will marry your daughter, Señora. You are obviously the true mother in law!"

6. MASCOTA DEL AÑO

En la clinica veterinaria, dos perros se quejan. El pastor aleman dice, "Son fregaderas, mano!"

El gran danesa pregunta, "¿Que pasó?"

El aleman dice, "Mi ama me sacó a la calle, vi a la perra del vecino, no me aquante y me le monté y me castrarán."

"Algo similar me pasó con mi ama, cuando se bañaba," cuenta el danesa, "Se agachó por jabón, no me aguante y...¡zas!"

"¡Ay, wey!" dice el aleman, "¿Te van a castrar, también?"

"Pues, no," contesta el danesa orgulloso, "¡Sólo a cortar las uñas!"

PET OF THE YEAR

In the veterinary clinic, two dogs are complaining. A German Shepherd says, "They're fuckers, bro!"

The Great Dane asks, "What happened?"

The shepherd says, "My owner took me out in the street, I saw the bitch next door, I couldn't stand it and mounted her and they're going to castrate me."

"Something similar happened with my owner, when she was bathing," said the Dane, "She bent over for the soap, I couldn't handle it and... pow!"

"Oh shit," said the German, "They going to castrate you, too?"

"Nah, " said the Dane proudly, "Just cut my nails."

7. El AMIGO

Eran cuatro tipos que estaban jugando dominó en un bar. Al rato de estar jugando, uno de ellos se levanta para ir al baño. Aprovechando el descanso, los demás se pusieron a charlar, y uno de ellos dijo: "No es por presumirles, pero a me hijo el ha ido muy bien en el negocio de bienes raíces. Ha ganado tanto dinero que ya hasta le ha regalado un condominio en Acapulco a uno de sus amantes."

El siguiente agrega: "Pero tampoco es por presumirles, pero me hijo es distribuidor de automóviles deportivos, y gana tanto dinero, que ya hasta le regaló un Ferrari a uno de sus ligas."

Y el tercero la remata con: "Pues mi hijo tiene una casa de la bolsa y como le han ido tan bien hasta le regaló a su amante un paquete de acciones de las mejores."

En eso llega el que estaba en el baño. Los tres presumidos les preguntan cómo le ha ido a su hijo, y el les responde: "Pues la verdad, mal. Mi hijo desde chico era medio delicadito, y ahora de mayor, se afeminó totalmente: es un homosexual declarado y trabaja en un salón de belleza.

"Pero ha de ser muy bueno lo que hace, porque uno de sus novios le regaló una condo en Acapulco, otro un Ferrari rosita, y otro un paquete de acciones de las más buenas."

THE BUDDY

There were four guys that had been playing dominoes in a bar, After playing awhile, one of them got up to go to the bathroom. Taking advantage of the break, the others started chatting, and one of them said: "I don't want to brag to you, but my son has done really well in the real estate business. He's made so much money that he even gave a condo in Acapulco to one of his lovers."

The next one added: "Well, I don't want to brag either, but my son is a sports car distributor and he made so much money that even gave a pink Ferrari to one of his lovers."

The third topped it with: "Well, my son has a brokerage house and it's doing so well that he even gave his main squeeze a portfolio of the top stocks."

At this point the guy who'd been in the bathroom got back. The three braggarts asked him how his son had been doing and he said: "Well, tell the truth, not so good. My son's been fairly sissy since he was little and now that he's grown up, he gone totally effeminate: he's an open homosexual and works in a beauty salon.

"But he must be really good at whatever it is he does, because one of his boyfriends gave him a condo in Acapulco, and another one a pink Ferrari, and another one a portfolio of the best stocks."

8. MAS O MENOS VALIDO

Un viejo menosvalido acerca una muchacha buenisima en el Metro, apoyado en sus maletas y presentando una lata para limosna.

Notando la forma muy guitarra de la chava, dice, "Ay, mamacita, curamela."

Ella, molesta, contesta enojada, "Cojo feo."

"No importa, chulis," responde el ruco, "Te enseño."

TOTALLY LAME

An old handicapped guy approaches a hot chick in the subway, leaning on his crutches and holding out a can for alms.

Noticing how built she is, he says, "Hey, little mama, how about it?"

Ticked off, she snaps, "Ugly cripple."

"Doesn't matter, cutie," the old guy says, "I'll teach you."

The pun here is that **cojo** means "cripple", but also means "I fuck" (first person of **coger**). So, "**Cojo feo**." also means"I fuck lousy."

Note **buena** for "hot", **ruco** for "old man", **metro** for "subway", **guitarra** (guitar) for "shapely", and **curamelo**, literally "cure me of it", but actually a very crude hit line.

9. LA OTRA

Una mujer enfrenta su esposa con quejas, "Me dijieron que andas con otra vieja."

Su marido contesta "Vieja, no. Tiene diecinueve años."

Mas enojada, su "jefa" dice, "Y que le pusiste "casa chica".

Hablando la verdad, dice, "Chica, no. Tiene alberca y frontón.

Pero siga con, "Tambien me enteré que comienzas dormir con ella."

Su esposa dice, "Dormir, no. Ella ni me deja dormir."

THE OTHER WOMAN

A woman confronts her husband with her complaints: "They say you've got another old lady."

Her husband answers, "What do you mean 'old?' She's only nineteen."

Even madder, the "boss lady" says, "And they say you set her up a "little house'." (A mistress' pad, as opposed to the wife's "casa grande")

Truthfully, the husband says, "What do you mean, 'little'? It's got a pool and tennis court."

But she keeps on, "And, I found out that you've been sleeping with her."

Her hubby says, "What do you mean 'sleeping' with her? She never lets me sleep."

10. TOMAR MEDIDAS

Una suculenta morra llega acompanada de un fortachon a su casa y preocupada dice a su mama: "Mami, estoy embarazada!"

Enfuriada, su mama dice, "Ay tonta caliente! No te dijé que tomarás medidas?"

"Y si eso hice," contesta la ingenua chava, "Tomé medidas y me quedé con la mas grande!"

TAKING MEASURES

A succulent girl comes home with her latest hunk and, obviously worried, says to Mother, "Mommy, I'm pregnant!"

Furious, her mom says, "Oh you horny little dummy! Didn't I tell you to take certain measures?"

"But I did," answers Miss Naivete, "I took measures and kept the biggest one."

HOMBRES=CERDOS   MEN ARE PIGS

En qué se diferencia un cerdo de un principe?
Cinco cervezas.

> What's the difference between a pig and a
> prince?
> Five beers.

Cómo se congela a un cerdo?
Jalandole la cobija.

> How do you freeze a pig?
> Hogging the covers.

Por qué no se casan las mujeres?
Les molesta que por cien gramos de chorizo se tienen
que llevar todo el cerdo.

> Why don't women get married? It bugs them that
> for 100 grams of sausage they have to get the
> whole pig.

21

Los hombres parecen las cervezas del botella porque del cuello para arriba sólo tienen aire.

> Men are like bottled beer because from the neck up they're just full of air.

Cuál es la forma mas facil de volver loco a un hombre en la cama?
Escondiéndole el control remoto.

> What's the easiest way to drive a man crazy in bed?
> Hide the remote.

Qué hace un hombre en la cama después de hacer el amor?
Estorbar.

> What does a man do in bed after making love?
> Gets in the way.

Qué hacen las mujeres mientras encuentran al hombre de su vida?
Se casan.

> What do women do until they meet the love of their life?
> Get married.

¿En qué se parecen los hombres a las medias?
En que sólo sirven para meter la pata.

How are men like stockings?
They're only good for putting a foot in it.

¿Por qué existen los hombres?
Porque un vibrador no te paga un trago.

>Why do men exist?
>Because a vibrator doesn't pay for drinks.

Definicion final de lo que es un hombre:
Conjunto de células medianamente organizadas que rodean a un pene.

>Definition of a man: A group of cells loosely organized around a penis.

En qué mes los hombres cometen menos estupideces?
En febrero, porque sólo tiene veinte ocho dias,

>In which month do men do less stupid things?
>February, because it only has 28 days.

Dicen las mujeres que lo ideal es un hombre 80-2-80. Es decir: 80 años de edad, 2 infartos, y 80 milliones de pesos.

>Women say that the ideal measurements for a man are 80-2-80. That is: 80 years old, 2 heart attacks, and 80 million pesos

¿Cual es la diferencia entre un bar y un clitoris?

Qualquier hombre encuentra un bar.

> What's the difference between a bar and a clitoris?
> Any man can find a bar.

Porque los hombres nunca sufren de la enfermedad de la vaca loca?

Poque son unos cerdos.

> Why don't men suffer from mad cow disease?
> Because men are pigs.

LA INDOMINABLE

Dos encamables amigas platican mientras caminar por una Plaza Comercial. Dice una, "¡Ay, Mana! ¡Todas las noches tengo que defenderme de los hombres con los que salgo!"

La otra, "No te han logrado hacer nada?"

Petulante contesta la primera, "¡Aun no! Por eso pienso salir con hombres más fuertes."

MISS INDOMINABLE

Two very "bedable" friends are talking while walking in the mall. One says, "Wow, honey! Every night I have to defend myself from the guys I go out with."

"Nobody's managed to 'do anything' yet?"

Pouting, the first babe answers, "Not yet! That's why I'm thinking of going out with stronger guys.

SUPERARSE

Una empleada doméstica pidió aumento de sueldo. A la señora no le sentió muy bien la solicitud, así que le preguntó: María, ¿por qué crees que mereces que te aumente el sueldo?

Señora, hay tres razones:La primera es que yo plancho la ropa mejor que usted.

¿Quién te ha dicho que planchas mejor que yo?

Su esposo, señora.

¡Oh, vaya!

La segunda razón es que yo cocino mejor que usted.

Eso es puro cuento, ¿quién te ha dicho que cocinas mejor que yo?

También su esposo, señora.

¡Ah, caramba!

Y la tercera razón, y la más importante, es que yo soy mejor que usted en la intimidad.

Al oírlo, la señora, completamente descompuesta y gritando le pregunta a la empleada:

¡¿Mi esposo te ha dicho eso?!

No, señora... me lo dijo el jardinero.

BETTER THAN

A housemaid asked for a raise in pay. The lady of the house didn't think much of the request, so she asked, "Why do you think you deserve my raising your pay?"

"Señora, there are three reasons. The first is that I iron better than you."

"Who told you that you iron better than I do?"

"Your husband, Señora."

"Oh, get real!"

"The second reason is that I cook better than you."

That's just not true. Who told you that you cook better than me?"

"Also your husband, señora."

"Oh, hell!"

"The third reason, and the most important, is that I'm better than you in the sack."

Hearing that, her mistress, totally upset and screaming, asked her, "Did my husband tell you that?"

"No, Señora... the gardener told me."

FRANCESITA

Un hombre que siempre molestaba a su mujer, pasó un día por la casa de unos amigos para que lo acompañaran al aeropuerto a dejar a su esposa que viajaba a París.

A la salida de inmigración, frente a todo el mundo, él le desea buen viaje y en tono burlón le grita:

¡¡Amor, no te olvides de traerme una hermosa francesita. Ja, ja, ja!!

Ella bajó la cabeza y se embarcó muy molesta. La mujer pasó quince días en Francia.

El marido otra vez pidió a sus amigos que lo acompañasen al aeropuerto a recibirla.

Al verla llegar, lo primero que le grita a toda voz es:

¡Mi amor, ¿¿me trajiste mi francesita??!

Hice todo lo posible -contesta ella- ahora sólo tenemos que esperar a ver si el bebé que tengo es niña.

FRENCH GIRL

A guy who always bugged his wife went by the house of some friends who would accompany them to the airport when he dropped off his wife, who was traveling to Paris.

At the emigration gate, in front of everybody, he wished her a nice trip and in a joking tone shouted, "Hey, love, don't forget to bring me back a beautiful little French girl. Ha, ha."

She lowered her head and boarded very ticked off. She spent fifteen days in France.

Her husband again asked their friends to go with him to the airport to meet her.

Seeing her arrive, the first thing he called out at the top of his lungs was, "My love! Did you bring me back a little French girl?"

"I did all I could," she answered. "Now we just have to wait and see if the baby is a girl or boy."

QUE JOROBA

Un calvo pasa por la calle y se cruza con uno que lleva joroba, y le dice: ¿Qué llevas en la mochila?

A lo que el jorobado le contesta: ¡Tu peine, imbécil!

JUST A HUNCH

A bald guy meets a hunchback and says, "What you got in the backpack?"

The hunchback answers, "Your comb, imbecile!"

ESPERANZA

Un Francés quería ir a un safari en el Yucatan y contrató a un guía Mexicano. Estando en plena selva apareció un tigre. El Mexicano huyó corriendo y el Francés le gritó: "¡Espera, espera!"

Y el Mexicano le responde, "¡No es perra, es tigre!"

WAIT UP

A Frenchman wanted to go on a safari in the Yucatan and hired a Mexican guide. Once in the jungle a tiger appeared. The Mexican took off running and the Frenchman yelled, "Wait, wait!"

The Mexican answered, "It's not a bitch, it's a tiger!"

The pun here is between **espera** (wait) and **es perra** (it's a female dog). The reason it's a Frenchman is that their accent tends to make an "r" sound more like the "rr" sound.

CIEN PERCENTO

Después del examen, la maestra llama a Pepito y le dice:

"¿No te da pena haber copiado integramente la prueba de Paquita Pecas?"

"¡No es cierto!" responde el cábula chamaco.

"Ah ¿No?" le increpa la maestra, todavia más enojada por su cinicismo, "Entonces ¿Por qué todas tus repuestas son iquales?"

"Pura coincidencia," le dice Pepito sin inmutarse.

"¡¿Y por pura coincidencia, en las pregunta doce donde Paquita respondió 'No lo sé', tu pusiste...'Yo tampoco'?!"

100 PERCENT

After the test, the teacher called Pepito up and said, "Aren't you ashamed of having completely copied from Paquita Pecas' paper?"

"Not true!" responds the bratty kid.

"Oh no?" scolds the teacher, even madder because of Pepito's cynicism. "Then why are your answers all the same as hers?"

"Pure coincidence," says Pepito, not giving an inch.

"And is it coincidence that on question twelve, where Paquita answered, 'I don't know', you put...'Me neither'?"

SORPRENDIENTE

Un reo escape del "bote" y se esconde en un convento, disfrazado en habito de monja.

Llegan las quardias para buscar y dijo a la madre superiora que deberia sucedir. Angustiada, ella lo explica de las monjitas: Tendremos ayudar, hijas. Todas haganse contra la pared, y cuando pasa el oficial, subanse el habito para enseñar que eres mujer, y digan su nombre.

Mucho verguenza, pero tuvieron que registrar una por una. La primera monja levanta su habito y dice: Sor…Ana.

La proxima, Sor… Helena.

Despues, Sor…Ayde.

Hasta la ultima, quien subió su falda e en voz baritono dijo, Sor…¡Presa!

SHOCKER

A prisoner escaped from the "can" and hid in a convent, disquised in a nun's habit.

The guards arrived to search and told the mother superior how it would work. Anguished, she explained it to the novitiates. "We have to assist them, Daughters. Everybody against the wall and when the officer passes raise your habit to show you are a woman, and say your name.

Great shame, but they had to do it, one after the other. The first non lifted her habit and said, "Sister Ana."

The next, "Sister Helena."

Then, "Sister Ayde."

Until the last one, who hiked up the skirt and in a baritone voice said, "Surprise!

This is a clever, multi-level pun. **Sor** is "Sister", but **sorpresa**! Is "surprise." But beyond that, **presa**, like **reo**, means "prisoner" or "inmate", so the "nun" is also saying, "Sister Prisoner".

SOR GROSERITA

Una monjita demasiado grosera estaba como interna en el convento del pueblo. Siempre que platicaba con sus compañeras, de cualquier cosa ella decía muchas leperadas.

Las demás ya estaban cansadas, hasta que en una conversación que tuvieron, llegaron a la conclusión de que cuando la monja grosera dijera una de sus cosas, la dejarían sola en el lugar en que estuvieran.

En una ocasión hablaban de la guerra y sus consecuencias, y una de ellas dijo: "Si yo pudiera, mandaría un camión lleno de alimentos para toda esa pobre gente que no tiene que comer".

Otra enunció: "Si yo pudiera, mandaría un camión lleno de medicinas para los pobres enfermos".

Y en eso dice la monja grosera: "Si yo pudiera, mandaría un camión lleno de putas para todos esos hijos de la Chingada".

De repente todas las monjas se paran de sus lugares, corren y se dirigen a la puerta, mientras la monja grosera les grita: "¡Espérense bola de tarugas, todavía ni contrato el camión!".

SISTER POTTYMOUTH

A very dirty-mouthed nun was an intern in the town convent. Whenever she talked with her companions about anything she used a lot of bad words.

The other nuns were tired of it, and in a discussion about it, came to the conclusion that whenever the foul-mouthed nun said one of her things, they'd quickly leave her presence.

One time they talked about the war and its consequences, and one of them said, "If I could, I'd send a truck full of food for all those poor people left with nothing to eat."

Another announced, "If I could, I'd send a truck full of medicine for the poor wounded."

Then the nasty monk said, "If I could, I send a truck full of whores for all those sons of bitches."

Quckly all the nuns left their places and ran towards the door while the nasty-mouth nun yelled, "Wait, you bunch of idiots, I haven't hired the truck yet."

In addition to **grosero** meaning not only "gross" and "dirty", but also "rude", note the form of **lepera**, which literally means "leper", but refers specifically to a potty-mouthed person, and their "unclean" trash talk as **leperadas**.

ME OFRESCO

Estaban unas monjas preparándose para ordenarse, haciendo una simulación de las palabras que ese día se pronunciarían.

Iban pasando una a una con el sacerdote al frente diciendo: "Padre, yo me ofrezco"..."Padre, yo me ofrezco"... "Padre, yo me ofrezco"... De pronto dice una de ellas: "Padre, yo me doy."

La madre superiora preocupada se acerca a ella y le dice: "Sor Bido, no se dice: yo me doy; tienes que decir igual que las demás hermanas: yo me ofrezco", y ella le responde angustiada: "No Madre, es que yo no meo fresco, ¡yo meo calientito y espumoso!"

OFFERING

There were some nuns preparing themselves to take Orders, rehearsing the words that they would speak on that day.

They were passing one by one in front of a priest saying "Father, I offer myself."... "Father, I offer myself"..."Father, I offer myself."... But suddenly one of them said, "Father, I give myself."

The mother superior, worried, came near her and said, "Sister Bido, you don't say 'I give myself,' you should say, 'I offer myself,' like all the other sisters." And she responded, anguished, "No Mother, it's because I don't pee cool. I pee warm and frothy."

The pun here is **me ofrezco** heard as **meo fresco**—"I piss cool"--from **mear**, meaning "to piss".

"**Sor Bido**" is "Sister Bido", a pun on **sorbido**, meaning to slurp or suckle.

POR EQIVOCACIÓN

Temprano se levanta la madre superiora y recorre el convento para ver que hacen sus discípulas monjas. Encontrando una en el corredór, dice: "Buen día Sor Inés, ¿cómo te sienta esta bella mañana?"

Contesta la monjita, "Bien, reverenda madre. Pero veo que usted se levantó del lado equivocado de la cama."

Aunque perpleja por el comentario, continua hasta la concina, donde dice, "Buen día, Sor Ye-Ye, te ves muy contenta."

"Si, madre," contesta, "Pero usted se levantó por el lado equivocado de la cama ¿No?"

Intrigada por los comentarios, busca a su asistenta, "Sor Dina, ¿tu crees que esta mañana, me haya levantado por el lado equivocado de la cama?"

"Si, reverenda madre," contesta la obedienta monja.

"Y cómo lo sabes?"

"Porque trae puestas las pantuflas del Cura Melo."

BY MISTAKE

The mother superior wakes up early and cruises the convent to see what her disciple nuns were doing. Meeting one of them in the corridor, she says, "Good day, Sister Inez, how do you feel this beautiful morning?"

The nun answers, "Good, reverend mother. But I see you got up on the wrong side of the bed."

Although perplexed by that comment, she continues to the kitchen, where she says, "Good day, Sister Ye-Ye. You look very happy."

"Yes, Mother," she answers, "But you got up on the wrong side of bed, no?"

Intrigued by these comments, she looks up her assistant, "Sister Dina, do you think I have gotten up on the wrong side of the bed this morning?"

"Yes, Reverend Mother," answers the obedient nun.

"And how do you know that?"

"Because you've got on Cura Melo's bedroom slippers."

PADRE NUESTRO

Llega una apeticible muchacha a la capilla de San Goloteo, famosa por sus milagros en fertilidad, y dice: " ¿Es cierto que resando aqui una Ave María, queda una embarazada?"

Contesta el sacerdote, "No, Señora, solamente con Padre Isimo, pero ya esta de vacaciones."

OUR FATHER

A tasty young woman arrives at the chapel of San Goloteo, famous for miracles of fertility, and says, "Is it true that saying a Hail Mary here will get you pregnant?"

The priest answers, "No, Señora, only with Father Isimo, but he's on vacation."

(A side joke here is that **Padrisimo** is slang for "very cool".)

TRAUMATIZADORA

Una buenérrima pero tímida jovencita llega al confesionario con Cura Melo y dice, "Padre, digame...¿Es cierto que la castidad causa traumas?"

Sabiendo de donde viene la pregunta, el cura contesta "Nada más a tu novio, Hijita."

MELOTRAUMA

A very built but timid young girl comes to confession with Father Melo and says, "Father, tell me...is it true that chastity causes trauma?"

Recognizing the source of the question, the priest answers, "Just for your boyfriend, my daughter."

PECADORA

Una pelirroja va hasta el confesionario:

¿Pecas, hija?

Sí padre, hasta las nalgas.

REDHEAD

A redhead goes to confession:

Have you sinned, my daughter?

Yes, father, right down to my ass.

41

The pun is from second person of **pecar**, meaning "to sin", and **pecas**, meaning "freckles".

ORALE

Una muchacha en el confesionario:

Ora, hija.

Son los dos y media, padre.

PRAYER TIME

A girl goes to confession and priest says: "Pray, my daughter."

She replies, "It's two thirty, Father."

He says **ora**, meaning "prayer", she hears **hora**, "hour", as if he's asking her what time it is.

CUENTANOS

El novio habla con su futuro suegro.

"Hola, vengo a pedir la mano de su hija."

"¿Y usted está en condiciones de mantener una familia?"

"Sí, señor, yo trabajo y si puedo..."

"¿Está seguro? ¡Mire que somos nueve!"

COUNTING ON YOU

The fiancé talks with his future father-in-law:

"Hello, I've come to ask for the hand of your daughter."

"And are you in a position to support a family?"

"Yes, sir, I work and I can..."

"Are you sure? Look, there are nine of us!"

LA BODA

Dice el Árabe, "En mi pais la novia no ve al novio antes de la boda."

Y el mexicano, "Huy, en mi pais muchas novias no ven al marido despues de la boda."

WEDDING

The Arab says, "In my country the bride doesn't see the groom before the wedding."

And the Mexican, "Hey, in my country a lot of brides don't see their husband after the wedding."

ESPERANZA

El galán dice al padre de la muchacha, "Señor, ¿Tendré algún esperanza con su hija?"

Contesta, "Ninguna, joven, ella ya decidió casarse con usted."

HOPEFUL

The suitor says to the father of the girl, "Sir, what hope would I have for your daughter?"

The father replies, "None. She's decided to marry you."

DIFFERENCIA

¿Cuál es la diferencia entre una novia y una esposa? 30 kilos.

What's the difference between a girlfriend and a wife?

50 pounds.

PORQUE?

Mamá, mamá... ¿por qué la novia va vestida de blanco?
Porqué es el momento más feliz de su vida.
¡Ah! ¿y por qué el novio va vestido de negro?

Mommy, mommy, why does the bride dress in white?

Because it's the happiest moment in her life.

Ah, then why does the groom dress in black?

TARDÓN

El jefe furioso le reclama a Don Tardencio Retardez, "Cómo es usted flojo, ya me enteré que llegó tarde hasta a su proprio matrimonio."

Responde Don Tardencio, "Sí, pero no lo sufficiente."

The furious boss scolded Don Tardencia Retardez. "You're so lazy, I found out you even arrived late at your own wedding."

"Not late enough."

DESHONORADA

Dos hermosas chicas con bikinis charlan el la playa, Según una, "A mí me deshonró mi novio y tuve que casarme."

Y la otra, "Pues yo deshonré a mi esposo y tuve que divorciarme."

Two beautiful chicks in bikinis chat at the beach. According to one, "My boyfriend dishonored me and I had to get married."

The other says, "Well, I dishonored my husband and had to get divorced."

Mothers In Law

Suegras

Epitafio en la tumba de una suegra: Aquí descansa ella. En casa descansamos todos.

>Epitaph on the tomb of a mother in law. "Here she rests in peace.   At home, all of us rest in peace.

-¡Auxilio, socorro, se quema la casaaa!
-¡Shhh! Silencio mi amor, no hagas ruido que vas a despertar a tu madre.

>Help, help, the house is on fire!
>Shhh! Silence, my love, don't make noise or you're going to wake up your mother.

¿Cuál es el castigo de la bigamia?
¡Tener dos suegras!

>What's the punishment for bigamy?
>Having two mothers in law.

Suegra a la nuera: ¿Por qué ese bebé no se parece a
su padre?
Bueno suegrita, yo tengo una cuca, no una
fotocopiadora!

Mother in law to daughter in law: Why doesn't
that baby look like his father?

Well, mama, I've got a pussy, not a photocopier.

Pepe, te veo preocupado.
Es que por poco atropello a mi suegra.
¿Te fallaron los frenos?
No, el acelerador.

Pepe, you look worried.

Because I almost ran over my mother in law.

Did your brakes fail?

No, my accelerator.

Durante el desayuno, la esposa comenta a su marido,
"Sí mi madre viene a vivir con nosotros tendremos que
mudarnos a una casa mas grande."

"¿Para que?" contesta su esposo, "Tarde o temprano
nos encontrará."

During breakfast, the wife says to her husband,
"If my mother comes to live with us we'll have to
move to a bigger house."

"Why?" her husband asks, "Sooner or later she'd
find us."

"Sancho" is a very Mexican personage: the guy who does your wife when you're not around. And, of course, there is also "Sancha."

LO MISMO

Dos amigos van por la calle, cuando de repente uno de ellos se para y exclama : Cielos! Mi mujer y mi amante vienen charlando hacia aqui!

Su amigo le mira con cara de estupefaccion y le dice : Coño! Yo iba a decir lo mismo!

THE SAME THING

Two friends are walking in the street when suddenly one of them stops and exclaims, "Omigod! My wife and my lover are coming this way talking to each other."

49

His friend looks stupefied, and says, "Damn! I was going to say the same thing."

COMO POLVO

Dice el juez, "A ver Don Cornelio. Por que se quiere divorciar de su mujer?"

"Porque trata a mis amigos como polvo, Licenciado."

"Ay caray! Y a que le llama usted tratarlos como polvo?"

"A que los esconde debajo de la cama."

LIKE DIRT

The judge says, "Let's see, Don Cornelio. Why do you want to divorce your wife?"

Because she treats my friends like dirt, Your Honor."

"Whoa! And what do you call 'treating them like dirt'?"

"She hides them under the bed."

PAGADO

Justo cuando el marido regresa sin previo aviso a casa, su mujer y el "Sanchez" estan juntando obligos en plena vista encima la mesa. Encabranado, el cornudo grita, "Maldito sancho! Por esto me lo vas a pagar."

Casualmente contesta el ya gozado, "Si me parece justo. Quanto cobras?

PAID UP

Just when the husband gets home without previous notice, his wife and "Sancho" are bumping navels in plain sight on the table. Pissed off, the cuckold cries, "Damned Sancho! You're going to pay for this!"

Casually, the recently satisfied guy answers, "Sounds fair to me. What do you charge?"

¿Cómo te fue en casa de tu novia?
Superbien. Fíjate que le caí bien a mis suegros, a mis cuñados, a las tías. El único que me miraba feo era su marido.

How did it go in your girlfriend's house?"

"Really well. Check it out, her parents liked me, her siblings, her aunts. The only one giving me dirty looks was her husband.

PRESENCIA PROFESIONÁL

Una vecina dice: Galina, estas enferma? Te lo digo porque he visto salir a un medico de tu casa esta mañana...

Mira, Macha, ayer por la mañana yo vi salir un coronel de la tuya y, sin embargo, no estamos en guerra.

PROFESSIONAL PRESENCE

The neighbor woman says, "Galina, are you sick? I ask because I saw the doctor coming out of your house early this morning."

The other woman says, "Look, Macha, yesterday morning I saw the colonel coming out of yours, but we're not having a war."

CUALQUIERA

Sorprendida por su marido mientras entretener al Sancho, la joven esposa dice, "Bueno sí, he sido debil, pero no con cualquiera.

Grita furioso su esposo, "¿Y que tiene de especial este hijo del la pinche chingada?"

"¡Ay!" la pecadora regaña, "No le digas asi que es tu compadre."

JUST ANYBODY

Surprised by her husband while entertaining "Sancho", the young wife says, "Okay, I've been weak, but not with just anybody."

Furious, her husband yells, "And what's so special about this damn son of a bitch?"

"Hey!" scolds the "sinner", "Don't talk about your best friend that way."

¿Cuál es la frase que más odia escuchar una esposa mientras esta haciendo el amor?
"¡Vieja, ya llegué!"

What's the phrase that a wife most hates to hear when she's making love?

"Honey, I'm home!"

AMBULANTE

Un paciente entra en la consulta del médico.

Doctor: - ¿Qué es lo que le ha traído por aquí?

Paciente - Una ambulancia, ¿por qué?

AMBULATORY

A patient enters the doctor's office.

Doctor: "What is it that's brought you here?"

Patient: "An ambulance. Why?"

AYUDITA

La ensabanable chica llega con su doctor y le dice, "La consulta no es para mí. Yo estoy bien."

El medico, impresionado, dice, "Ya lo veo. ¿Pero, entonces?"

"El que la necesita es mi marido." dice la chava averagonzada, "Ultimamente como ya no....usted entiende...bueno, es que quiero que paresca toro. ¿Me puede ayudar?"

"Claro que sí," contesta el doc, "Desnúdese, acuéstese en ese sofá y para comenzar vamos fabricandole los cuernos."

HELPFUL

A luscious chick goes to her doctor and says, "I'm not here about me. I'm fine."

The doctor, very impressed, says, "I can see that. What, then?"

"It's my husband that needs it," says the girl, embarrassed, "Lately he can't....you understand...well, I want him to be like a bull. Can you help me?

"Of course," answers the doc, "Strip and lay down on the couch and we'll start by putting the horns on him."

GONOCOCO

Despues de revisar los analisis, el Doctor se acerca a la potable paciente y dijo, "Señora, lamento decirle, pero usted tuvo contacto con un gonococo."

"Ah, si? Y eso mentiroso juro que aleman!"

GONORRHEA

After checking the test results, the Doctor approached the sexy patient and said, "Madam, I'm sorry to tell you, but you have had contact with a gonococcus."

"Oh, really? The liar swore he was a German."

TENDENCIAS

"Doctor, doctor, tengo tendencias suicidas, ¿qué hago?"

"Págueme ya mismo."

TENDENCIES

"Doctor, doctor, I have suicidal tendencies. What should I do?"

"Pay me right now."

RESULTADOS POSITIVOS

Leyendo los resultados de una prueba, el ginocologo dijo a su paciente (increiblemente, tambien ensanable) "Le tengo muy buenas noticias, Señora."

Confusa, la morra dijo, "No, Doc. Soy yo señorita."

"Entonces," siquio el medico sin pausa, "Le tengo muy malas noticias, Señorita."

POSITIVE RESULTS

After reading her test results, a gynecologist said to his patient (incredibly, also very sexy) "I have good news for you, Mrs. Brown."

Confused, the girl said, "No, Doc, It's Miss Brown."

"Well then," the doctor continued without missing a beat, "I've got bad news for you, Miss Brown."

CONSEJO

Al su muy traqueteado, pero dado de alta paciente, el galeno le recomienda, "Recuerde que por un tiempo dejara de fumar, y nada de viejas ni copitas, ni comes in restaurantes caros, ni nada de desvalados ni vacaciones."

La esposa del paciente dice, "Hasta que este bien de salud?"

Pero el doctor dice, muy estricto, "No. Hasta que acabe de pagarme."

ADVICE

To his very shook up, but official, patient, the doctor recommends, "Remember: no smoking for awhile, no women or drinking, don't eat in expensive restaurants or take any long vacations."

The patient's wife says, "Until his health gets better?"

But the doctor, very strict, says, "No. Until he pays off my bill."

Note **galeano** (Gallilean) for "doctor"... a weird, Biblical usage, but common in newspapers. **Dado de alta** can mean anything from "discharged" to "accepted".

SYMPTOMATICA

Despues de su revision, el Doc dice, "No puedo encontrar la razón de su enfermedad. Quizá sea causa de la bebida."

El paciente dice enojado, "En este caso, doctor, ya volveré cuando esté usted sobrio."

SYMPTOMATIC

After the examination, the Doc says, "I can't find any reason for your illness. Maybe its because of drinking."

The patient angrily replies, "In that case, Doctor, I'll come back when you're sober."

ESPUTA

Doctor, mi hija no se encuentra bien.
Dígame, ¿su hija esputa y excrementa?
Mi hija es puta, pero la otra, no.

ELIMINATION

Doctor, my daughter isn't well.

Tell me, does she spit and defecate?

Yeah, she's a whore, but not the other thing.

Esputa=spit. **Es puta**=is a whore. So, "She's a whore, but not crap."

LA CUENTA

El doctor dice a su arrugado paciente, "Usted ha bebido demasiado, y esto le ha perjudicado. ¿Cuántos años tiene?"

Responde el anciano, "Sesenta, doctor."

Aclara el médico, "¿Ve usted? Si no hubiese bebido tanto, ya tendria por lo menos ochenta."

WHO COUNTS?

The doctor says to his wrinkled patient, "You've done too much drinking, and it's ruined your health. How old are you?"

The old guy says, "Sixty, Doctor."

The doctor declares, "You see? If you hadn't drunk so much, you'd be at least eighty."

PASO POR PASO

Una ñora ya entrada en años comenta apenada al doctor, su embarazozo problema:

"Ya no soporto esta situación," dice, "Me pedorreo todo el tiempo."

Sigue, "Afortunadamente, nadie se da cuenta porque son ventosos silenciosos y sin olor. Es más, desde que empezamos a hablar me he echado más de veinte pedorrines. ¿Qué puedo hacer?"

El "doc" receta, "Tenga estas píldoras, tómese tres diarias y venga a verme dentro de una semana."

A la semana, la ñora regresa furiosa y le dice, "¡Doctor! No sé lo que tenían las píldoras que me dio, pero ahora el problema es peor. Me estoy tirando cuetes tanto como antes y todos son silenciosos, pero pestan horrible. Cómo se explica eso, Doctor?"

"Calmese, señora," dice el medico, escribiendo otra receta, "Ahora que ya le curé el olfato, le voy a recetar algo para la sordera."

ONE STEP AT A TIME

An old babe well advanced in years shyly tells her doctor about her embarrassing problem, "I can't stand this situation," she says, "I fart all the time."

"Fortunately, nobody notices because my 'wind' is silent and odorless," she goes on, "There's more, since we've been talking I've let more than twenty farts. What can I do?"

The Doc prescribes, "Take these pills, take three a day, and come see me within a week."

A week later, the old doll comes back, furious, and says, "Doctor! I don't know what's in those pills you gave me, but now the problem is worse. I'm 'shooting rockets' as much as before, and they're silent, but now they stink horribly. How do you explain that, Doctor?"

"Calm down, ma'am," says the doctor, writing another prescription, "Now that we've cured your sense of smell, I'm going to give you something for that deafness."

LO BUENO/ LO MALO

El doctor llama por teléfono a su paciente: "Vera, tengo una noticia buena y otra mala."

"Bueno... dígame primero la buena."

"Los resultados del análisis indican que le quedan 24 horas de vida."

"Pero, bueno, ¿eso es la buena noticia? ¿Entonces cuál es la mala?"

"Que llevo intentando localizarle desde ayer."

GOOD NEWS/BAD NEWS

The doctor calls his patient by telephone:

"Vera, I have good news and bad news."

"Well then, . . . tell me the good news first."

"The results of the analysis indicate that you have 24 hours left to live."

"Well, that's the good news? Then what's the bad news?"

"That I have been trying to reach you since yesterday."

A LA VISTA

"Doctor, doctor, veo elefantes azules por todas partes."

"Ha visto ya a un psicólogo ?"

"No, sólo elefantes azules."

SEEING BLUE

"Doctor, doctor, I see blue elephants everywhere."

"Have you seen a psychologist yet?"

"No, just blue elephants."

ASPECTO

Un matrimonio visita al médico. El médico le dice al marido, "Oye, no me gusta el aspecto de su esposa." Señor: "¡Ni a mí! Pero es que su padre es rico."

LOOKING BAD

A couple visited the doctor. The doctor said to the husband, "Listen, I don't like the way your wife looks."

The hubby: "Me neither. But her father's rich."

Waiting tables is, for some reason, considered a big deal profession in Mexico. Mexican waiters are also world famous for very slow service

BARRATO

Un cliente grita a un mesero, "Meserooooooooo...¡Hay una mosca muerto en mi plato!"

Con calma contesta, "¿Qué esperaba por ese precio, una viva?"

CHEAP

A customer yells at a waiter, "Waaaaaaiter! There's a dead fly in my soup!"

Calmly, the waiter replies, "What do you expect for that price, a live one?"

SERVICIO DE MAS ALLA

Una viuda va con una espiritista para que comunicar con el difunto. Apaga la luz y pone las manos en el velador, invocando al espiritu, pero trancurre un largo rato sin que la mesa se mueva.

"Su esposo no quiere contestar."

"Tenga paciencia. Era mesero."

TRANSCENDANT SERVICE

A widow goes to a spiritualist to communicate with the dead. She turns off the light and puts her hands on a candlestick, invoking the spirit, but a long time passes without the table moving.

"Your husband doesn't answer."

"Be patient. He was a waiter."

BUEN PROVECHO

En un restaurante, un cliente grita histerico, "¡Mesera, mesera!"

Muy ocupada, la muchacha dice, "¿Qué?"

"¿Me dejará sin comer, toda la noche?" grita el tipo.

"Claro que no," conesta ella, "Cerramos a las nueve."

BON APPETIT

In a restaurant, a custumer yells hysterically,
"Waitress! Waitress!"

Very busy, the girl says, "What?"

"Are you going to leave me without any food all night?"
the guy yells.

"Of course not," she replies, "We close at nine."

RELLENO

Oye, el cliente dice que su tortilla tiene hongos – grita
la mesera – Que hago?

Contesta el cocinero – Cobrale una quesadilla.

FILLING

Hey, this customer says his tortilla has fungus (or...
mushrooms) on it –the waitress yells -- what should I
do?

The cook answers – Charge him for a quesadilla.

SIGNIFICANCIA

Llama un cliente del restaurant de poco postín,
"¡Mesero! Una mosca en mi café. ¿Qué significa
esto?"

Poco preocupado, el mozo contesta, "No lo sé, Señor,
pero a lado hay una gitana que interprete aspectos y
signos. ¿Se la mando traer?

MEANING

A customer in a not-so-fancy restaurant calls out,
"Waiter! There's a fly in my coffee. What's the
meaning of this"?

Not too worried, the waiter answers, "I don't know, Sir,
but there's a gypsy next door who interprets signs and
omens. Shall I call her?

CLIMATÓLOGO

Cuando le ponen el plato al frente, el cliente anciano
exclama molesto, "Oigame, joven, esta sopa esta fria."

Igual de molesto, contesta el mesero, "Cómo lo sabe,
si aún no la ha probado?"

Indicandole con su dedo, dice el viejo, "Porque la
mosca está titiritando de frio!"

WEATHER REPORT

As soon as the waiter puts the dish in front of him, the old customer, very bothered, exclaims, "Listen young man, this soup is cold."

Equally upset, the waiter retorts, "How can you tell, since you haven't tried it yet?"

Pointing his finger, the old coot says, "Because the fly is shivering."

GALLEGOS Y GUASABENSES

Just as Americans joke about the stupidity of "Polacks" or "Aggies" in Texas, Spanish "stupid" jokes target "Gallegos" (natives of Galicia) for some reason. In Mexico, many such jokes are about Guasavenses, residents of Guasave, Sinaloa.

DIEZ Y MAZ

¿Por qué los gallegos siempre andan con la bragueta abierta?

Por si tienen que contar hasta once.

TEN AND MORE

Why do Gallegos always go around with their zippers open?

In case they have to count to eleven.

INOXIDABLES

Dos Gallegos, haciendo un paseo del ciudad, pasan a lado de una fabrica con letrero grande que dice, ACEROS INOXIDABLES.

Leyendolo, Venancio dice a su amigo, "¿Nos hacemos?"   .

STAINLESS

Two Gallegos, walking around the city, pass beside a factory with a big sign that says, "STAINLESS STEELS"

Reading it, Venancio says to his friend, "Should we make ourselves stainless?"

The pun is between **Aceros** for "steels" and **hacer os**, meaning "make yourselves"

DOMICILIO

In Guasave hay un letrero que dice, "Se pintan casas al domicilio."

HOME SERVICE

There's a sign in Guasave that says, "We paint houses: service at your home."

INVENTOS GALLEGOS

El aire acondicionada para motocicletas
El sartén de plástico
El Macho Ligero de aluminio
La toalla impermeable
Reloj de sol fosforescente para leer de noche

GALLEGO INVENTIONS

Air conditioning for motorcycles
The plastic frying pan
The lightweight aluminum sledgehammer
The waterproof towel
The phosphorescent sundial, for use at night

¿COMO?

Dos Gallegos platicando:

Manolo, ¿y cómo hace el amor tu esposa?
Pues ya no se Venancio, unos dicen que bien y otros
dicen que mal.

HOW SO?

Manolo, how does your wife make love?

I don't know, Venancio, some say good and others say
bad.

POR ADENTRO

Dos Gallegos estaban caminando en puro campo de Galicia, cuando un pajaro defecó en la cabeza de Venancio.

"Oye, Manolo" preguntó a su cuate, "¿Que tiene mi cabeza?"

Mirandole bien es sitio desecrada, dijó, "Pues...caca."

"Ay no, estupido," exclamó Venancio, "¿Que tengo por afuera?"

INSIDE

Two Gallegos were walking in the Galicia countryside when a bird defecated on Venancio's head.

"Listen, Manolo," he asked his pal, "What's with my head?"

Taking a good look at the desecrated site, he said, "Well....shit."

"No, stupid, "Venancio exclaimed, "What's on the outside?"

Era tan tonto que no sabia que su radio AM también servía pasado el medio día.

He was so stupid he didn't know his AM radio also worked in the afternoon.

TONTILANDIA

Llega un tontilandés a la farmacia y le pregunta al dependiente:
¿Tiene condones?
De los Sico?
No, de los del pito

STUPIDLAND

A dumbass arrives at the pharmacy and asks the clerk, "Do you have condoms?"

"Sico brand?"

"No, the ones for your dick."

Sico is a well-known brand of condoms in Mexico, like calling them Trojans. The pun is that the dunce understood, **de lo Sico** (of the Sico brand) for **Del hocico**, (for the snout or mouth) Note the **-landés** ending, making the guy a "Stupidese".

SOY YO

Venancio el Gallego fue a Mexico en viaje de negocios. En el taxi del aeropuerto el taxista supo que su cliente fue de Galicia y propuso una rompecabesa: "Que persona tiene los mismos padres que yo, pero no es mi hermana, ni mi hermano?"

Pensandolo profundamente, Venancio tuvo que rinderse, "Pue, no ze. Quien?"

Riendose, el chofer dijo, "Pues, yo!"

El Gallego fue tan impresionado con esa muestra de humor e intelligencia, que cuando regreso del Galicia, pregunto de sus amigos, "A ver, diganme...quien es alguien que no es ni mi hermana ni mi hermano pero tiene los mismos padres que yo?

Sacando su poca materia gris, los gallegos admitieron que no pueden contestar, y dijeron, "Jode, que no sabemos. Quien es?"

Riendo como mula, el Gallego grito, "Pues..un taxista en la ciudad de Mejico!"

IT'S ME

Venancio, the Gallego, went to Mexico on a business trip. In the taxi from the airport, the driver knew that his fare was from Galicia and asked him a riddle: "Who has the same parents as me, but isn't my sister or brother?"

Thinking deeply, Venancio had to give up, "Well, I dunno. Who?"

Laughing, the driver said, "Well, me!"

The Gallego was so impressed by this example of humor and intelligence that when he got back to Galicia, he asked his friends, "Let's see, tell me....who is it that isn't my brother or sister, but has the same parents as me?"

Wracking their little grey matter, the Gallegos admitted that they couldn't answer and said, "Fuck, we don't know. Who is it?"

Laughing like a donkey, Venancio yelled, "Well...a taxi driver in Mexico city!"

POR "PLIS"

Un gallego viaja en un crucero por el caribe pero como el barco es muy grande se pierde. "¡Rediez!" dice, "¿'On'toy?"

Pero aparece un oficial del barco y el gallego dice, "Dígame...donde ezta el camarote 1450?"

Con cortez, el oficial contesta, "Por babor, Señor."

Enojado, el gallego dice, "Eztá bien. Por babor, me podeiz dezir donde eztá el camarote 1450?"

PLEASE

A Gallego takes a Caribbean cruise, but because the ship is so big, he gets lost. "Jeez!" he says, "Where am I?"

But a ship's officer appears and the Gallego says, "Tell me, where is Cabin 1450?"

Courteously, the officer answers, "To port, Sir."

Miffed, the Gallego says, "OK. PLEASE, can you tell me where cabin 1450 is?"

Babor is the word for the port side of a ship (opposite of **estribor**). So the **b/v** confusion of Spanish and Gallego accent lead to confusing with **favor**.

LEMAS PARA CANTINAS

Si toma por olvidar, paque por adelante.
Evite la cruda, permanesca borracho.
Mas vale un borracho conocido que un Alcoholico Anonimo
Fracasé por quatro razones: el IVA, la uva, la eva, y el huevo.

SLOGANS FOR BARS

If you drink to forget, pay in advance.
Avoid hangover, stay drunk.
Better a well-known drunk than an anonymous alcoholic.
I failed for four reasons: the value added tax, drinking, women, and laziness.

(IVA is **Impuesto Valor Agregado, Uva** means "grape", and thus "wine" and thus "alcohol". Eva is "Eve" and thus all women. **El Huevo**, a Mexicanism harder to translate, refers to "balls", but signifys laziness.

SAMARITANO

Entrando su favorita cantina para chuparse unas chelas, Timoteo tropieza con un tipo que está tirado en el piso, bien pedo. Con mucho trabajo, lo pone de pie y, muy satisfecho por su buena acción, se sienta, pero el tipo vuelve al piso, poniendose murado su cara con el impacto.

De nuevo, Timoteo lo pone de pie y apenas da la vuelta, el cuate vuelve azotar. Y cuando nuevamente lo levanta, ya desangrando, le dice al cantinero, "Diga, este tipo está hasta las manitas... ¿Por qué no lo manda a su casa?" Pero el cantinero dice, "Porque no se donde vive."

Entonces, Timoteo revisa los bolsillos y de su cartera saca una identificación, y despues de leer lo, piensa, "¡Hijoles! Es hasta el otro lado de la ciudad."

Pero, como buen samaritano que es, se lo echa al hombro y lo sube a su auto y lo lleva hasta su casa, donde lo baja y recarga en la pared. Y cuando lo suelta, va de nuez al besar el banqueta.

Lo levanta otro vez y en esta momento, se abre la puerta y sale una chava, gritando, "¡Mi marido!"

Timoteo dice, alivio, "Que gusta me da oir eso, Señora. Tomelo."

La mujer, mirando su ya herido y ensangrentado esposo, dice, "Gracias por traerlo, joven. Pero...¿Dónde está su silla de ruedas?"

GOOD SAMARITAN

On the way into his favorite bar to toss back a few beers, Timoteo trips over a guy sprawled on the floor, totally shitfaced. With much dificulty, he puts him on his feet and, very satisfied with his good deed, sits down, but the guy falls down again, bruising his face on the floor.

Timoteo stands him up again, but as soon as he turns around, the guy falls over again. So when he stands him up again, Timoteo says to the bartender, "Hey, this guy's had it. Why don't you send him home?" But the bartender says, "Because I don't know where he lives."

So Timoteo searches the guy's pockets and finds an ID in his wallet, but after reading it thinks, "Jesus! It's all the way on the other side of town!"

But, like the good Samaritan he is, he shoulders the guy and carries him to his car, then takes him to his house, where he takes him out and stands him up against the wall. And when he lets go, the guy kisses the pavement again.

He's picking him up one more time when the door opens and a chick comes out yelling, "My husband!"

Timoteo, with relief, says, "I'm really glad to hear that, Señora. Take him."

But the woman, looking at her by now beatup and bleeding husband, says, "Thanks for bringing him home, young man. But...where's his wheelchair?"

FRONTERIZO UNO

Despues muchos dificultares, los Oaxacos Chucho y Ignacio llegaron al cerco que marca la frontera de los Estados Unidos. Despues de pensar sobre la problema un rato, digo Chucho, "Oye, compa, tu levantas el alambre asi que puedo cruzar. Entonces, yo lo levantare para que cruces tu."

Dicho es hecho, y mientras Nacho apoya el alambre, Chucho cruza muy facil, llegando al otro lado y por alla para, mirando a un lado y al otro.

"Epa, Pedrito, " llamo Nacho, "Ya toca a ti." Pero Chucho no hace nada.

"Ay, wey," grita Nacho, "Levanta al alambre, asi que podria cruzar."

Fijando en el, Chucho toca su oreja y dice, "What?"

BORDER JOKE # 1

After many difficulties, the two Oaxacans Chucho and Ignacio arrived at the fence that marks the border of the United States. After thinking about the problem awhile, Chucho says, "Listen, pal, you lift the wire so I can cross under it. Then I'll lift it from the other side so you can cross."

No sooner said than done, and while Nacho holds up the wire, Chucho crosses easily. On the other side, he stops, looking around from one side to the other.

"Hey Chucho," Nacho calls, "Now it's your turn." But Chucho doesn't do anything.

"Hey, turkey," Nacho yells, "Lift the wire so I can get across."

Looking at him, Chucho touches his ear and says, (In English) "What?"

FRONTERIZO DOS

Les costó mucho, pero Chucho y Ignacio por fin brincaron hasta los Estados Unidos. Pero despues de todo el ejercicio y miedo, Nacho tuve mucho ganas de defecar.

"Ay, Chucho," dijo, "Donde puedo zurrar?"

"Por a'i en los arbustos," contestó su amigo.

Despues Nacho grito, "Ay, Chucho. Como voy a limpiar el culito?"

"Pos, con piedritas," contesto Chucho.

Al repente, viene La Migra, muy sospechosos. A Chucho contestaron, muy pesados, "Jei, usted. Donde nació?"

Dijo Chucho, "Está cagando."

La Migra siguio, "Y tiene papeles?"

"Pos, no," dijo Chucho, "Por eso está limpiandose con piedras."

BORDER JOKE # 2

It was tough, but Chucho and Ignacio finally "jumped" to the United States. But after all that exercise and fear, Nacho really had to take a dump.

"Hey, Chucho," he said, "Where can I shit?"

"Over there in those bushes," Chucho replied.

A few minutes later, Nacho yelled, "Hey, Chucho. How am I going to wipe my ass?"

Chucho said, "Well, use some pebbles."

Suddenly, the Border Patrol appeared, very suspicious of Chucho. "Hey, you," they asked, coming on very heavy, "Where were you born?"

Chucho said, "He's taking a shit."

The Border Patrol agent pressed on, "Have you got papers?"

"Well, no," Chucho said, "That's why he's wiping himself with rocks."

When asked **Donde nació**? (Where were you born?) Chucho hears **Donde Nacho**? (Where's Nacho?)

FRONTERIZO TRES

(Se entiende que La Migra tiene muchas problemas en distinquir los Mexicanos illegales de los "chicanos" o "Latinos" quienes son legales.)

Entonces, cuando encuentra cerca la frontera una joven indita, el agente pregunta, "Tu, señorita, eres Latina?"

"Uy no, siñor," contesta la indita, "Yo soy La Lupe. La Tina ya se fue a Los Angeles."

BORDER JOKE # 3

(Understanding that a major problem for the Border Patrol is telling illegal Mexicans from the legal "Chicanos" or "Latinos".)

So, when he runs across a young Mexican Indian girl near the border, the agent asks, "You, Miss. Are you a Latina? (Are you La Tina?)

"Oh, no sir," the indita answers, "I'm La Lupe. La Tina just left for Los Angeles."

The "Siñor is hick accent. The "La" before a woman's name is not uncommon, generally seen as low class.

Bilingual Jokes
Chistes Bilingues

Bilingual jokes are my favorite kind. These can mostly be told in either Spanish or English, but require that the listener speak both languages.

¿QUE?

Un Tejano, en viaje a Ciudad Juarez entra un bar "de trabajadoras" y choca con una re-buena y sexy. Impresionado, dice, "Beibi, te quiero coger."

Ella no habla Inglés, y responde, "¿Mande?"

El Tejano grita, "No, hoy!"

HUH?

A Texan visitng Juarez walks into a "working girl" bar and immediately bumps into a very hot number. Impressed, he says, "Baby, I want to fuck you,"

Not speaking English, she says, "¿Mande?"

The Texan bellows, "No, today!?

Pun on **mande**, meaning "huh?", and "Monday."

TIEMPO DE NIEVE

Un Mexicano que trabaja en Chicago pasa por un campo de nieve y necesita miar. Entonces saca su pistola y, al pesar del frio, comienza regar el hielo.

Un gringo pasa y lo saludo con su mano, y dice, "Pretty chilly."

Contesta el Mexicano, "Gracias. Muy amable"

SNOWY WEATHER

A Mexican guy who works in Chicago is crossing a snowy field and has to piss. So he pulls it out, in spite of the cold, and starts watering the ice.

An American passes and waves at him, and says, "Pretty chilly."

The Mexican answers, "Thanks. Very kind."

The Mexican is hearing "chilly" as **chile**, a common word for "dick" or "cock", so he takes the compliment.

SOCKS

A Latino man who spoke no English went went to buy socks in a department store. He told the clerk, "Quiero calcetines."

"I don't speak Spanish, but we have some very nice suits over here." said the salesgirl.

"No, no quiero trajes. Quiero calcetines." said the man.

She held up some shirts, but he said, "No quiero camisas. Quiero calcetines." repeated the man.

So she showed him some slacks.

"No, no quiero pantalones. Quiero calcetines." insisted the man.

She pointed to underpants.

"No quiero calzones. Quiero calcetines."

"How about some undershirts?" She was starting to lose her patience.

"No quiero camisetas. Quiero calcetines."

Suddenly he saw some socks on a table and grabbed a pair, exclaiming, "Eso si que es!".

"Well, if you could spell it, why didn't you say so in the first place?" asked the exasperated salesgirl.

"**Eso si que es**" means "that's it"… say it aloud to get the joke.

VISTA

Dos marineros--uno frances y el otro Mexicano-- trabajan en un barco de pasajeros.

Como de costumbre, muchos de los pasajeros hacen ejercicio en la cubierta por la mañana. Un dia, los dos amigos miran a una pasajera lindisima corriendo por la cubierta.

De repente, llega un gran viento, y se le levanta la falda corta a la muchacha, dandoles a los marineros una vista magnifica de su cucu bonito.

El frances da un suspiro, se besa los dedos y dice, "Ah, c'est la vie!"

El Mexicano responde, "Se la vi tambien."

VISION

Two sailors—one French and one Mexican—worked on a passenger ship.

As always, many of the passengers exercised on the deck in the morning. On day the two frineds saw a very pretty passnger running on the deck.

Suddenly a big wind came up and blew up the girl's short skirt, giving the sailors a magnificent view of her pretty pussy.

The Frenchman signed, kissed his fingers, and said, "Ah, c'est la vie!"

The Mexican answered, "I saw it, too."

LA PUSIERA

A Mexicana in Los Angeles speaks no English, boards a bus. She drops a coin in the box, but the driver doesn't see her do it.   He points to the box and says, "Hey, lady... put your money in the hopper."

She says, "**Ya lo puse**." (I already put it in)

He says, "Put your coins in the slot, lady!"

Annoyed, she snaps louder, "**Ya lo puse**!"

Irritated, the driver yells back, "I don't care if it's green with purple pubies—put your money in the box."

Ya lo pusé means "I already put it:... say it aloud to get it.

PAISANO INTÉRPRETE

En Estados Unidos un mexicano busca un amigo también mexicano para que lo ayude en la traducción con un doctor.

Ya en el consultorio del doctor

Doctor - What's wrong with your friend?

Amigo - Dice el doctor ¿Qué es lo que tienes?

Mexicano - Dile que me duele en medio de las paletas y el dolor me sube hasta la sien.

Amigo - He says that his popsicles hurt in the middle and it goes up to one hundred!

Doctor - What else?

Amigo - ¿Qué mas tienes?

Mexicano - Las muñecas me duelen mucho en las mañanas.

Amigo - He says his dolls hurt very much in the mornings.

Doctor - Tell your friend he is mentally retarded.

Amigo - El doctor dice que te pongas mentolato por las tardes.

HOMEBOY INTERPRETS

A Mexican in the U.S. looks up a Mexican friend to help him translate to a doctor.

In the doctor's office it goes like:

Doctor - What's wrong with your friend?

Friend – The Doc asks what brings you here.

Mexican patient - Tell him it hurts in the between my shoulder blades and the pain goes up to my temple.

Friend - He says it hurts between his popsicles and the pain goes up to a hundred!

Doctor - What else?

Friend - What else is bothering you?

Mexican patient – My wrists hurt a lot in the mornings.

Friend - He says his dolls hurt very much in the mornings.

Doctor - Tell your friend he is mentally retarded.

Friend - The doctor says put on mentholate in the evenings.

Obviously this one works on a series of double-meanings. **Paleta** is a shoulder blade as well as a popsicle. (Not to mention a palette, trowel, ladle, front tooth, flank steak, and many other things.) **Sien** is temple, but pronounced just like **cien**, meaning "hundred". **Muñeca** means both doll and wrist. The jump from "mentally retarded" to applying menthol in the evening is sloppier, but funny—the similarities of words should be obvious.

BELÉN

En Nochebuena, una guardia Israeli, en su puesto cerca de Belén vea acercando una pereja de Arabes. La mujer, montada en un burro, está embarazada. Dice "¿Quien vive?"

Contesta el hombre, "Jose, y mi esposa Maria."

"¿Porque queren pasar? "

"Vamos a Belen, donde mi marida var a dar un luz."

"Ah, ¿si? ¿No te pareces extraño? ¿Maria, Jose, Belen, Nochebuena? Supungo que van a poner al niño 'Jesus'."

"Claro que no! Somos Arabes, no Mexicanos. "

BETHLEM

On Christmas eve, an Israeli guard at his post near Bethlehem sees an Arab couple approaching. The woman, mounted on a burro, is pregnant. He says, "Who goes there?"

93

The man answers, "Joseph, and my wife Mary."

"Why to you want to enter?"

"We're going to Bethlehem where my wife can have her baby."

"Oh, yeah? Doesn't that seem strange? Mary, Joseph, Bethlehem, Chrismas Eve? I suppose you're going to call the kid Jesus?"

"Of course not! We're Arabs, not Mexicans."

This one works better told in English.

CUENTO NAVIDEÑO

Como a su galán se pasó la mano en el brindis navideño, y a la mera hora se queda jetón, Rebeca Liente está furiosa. "¡Imbecil!" grita, ¿Es la 'Noche Buena' que me prometió? No me quedaré asi. ¡Necesito un hombre!"

Y estaba a mitad del berrinche, cuando escuchó ruidos provientes de la sala, y al investigar discrubre, el mero "Santa Clos".

Acercando al "Santa" gordito, dice "Espera Santita, No te vayas. ¿Qué te ofrezco leche y galletas?"

Pero Santa dice, "Nada, mi hija. Tengo que irme con los niños del mundo."

Muy coqueta, dice Rebeca, "¿Ni un vinito para frio? Anda, quedate.¿Si?"

Pero Santa dice, "Me voy. Los niños del mundo me esperan."

Poniendose mas directa, dice la muchacha, "¿Algo mas fuerte? Tengo cognac."

Pero Santa dice, "Me voy. Ya mero amanece."

Quitando su bata y tocando Santa con sus tetas desnudas, la muy piruja dice, "En ese caso, si no tienes ni sed ni hambre, ¿Tu y yo nos ponemos comodos?"

Santa dice, "No, me voy, me voy....."

Pero ella sigue cariciandole hasta que Santa, viendose por abajo, dice, "Ya tengo que quedarme. ¡Ahorita ni quepo por la chimenea!

CHRISTMAS TALE

Since her boyfriend has passed out from Christmas toasts and at the moment remains blotto, Rebeca Liente is furious. "Moron!" she yells, "Is this the 'Christmas Eve' you promised me? I'm can't handle this. I need a man!"

And halfway through her tantrum, she hears providential noises in the living room and, upon investigating discovers none other than Santa.

Nearing the chubby "Saint", she says, "Wait, Santy. Don't leave. Can I offer you milk and cookies?"

But Santa says, "Nothing, honey. I have to go see the children of the world."

Flirtatiously, she says, "Not even some wine for the cold. Come on, stay awhile, OK?"

But Santa says, "I'm leaving. The children of the world expect me."

Getting more direct, she says, "Something stronger? I've got cognac."

But Santa says, "I have to go. Dawn is coming."

Throwing off her bathrobe and touching Santa with her naked tits the little slut says, "In that case, if you're not hungry or thirsty, let's get comfortable."

Santa says, "No, I'm leaving, I'm leaving..."

But she keeps stroking until Santa, glancing down at himself, says, "I have to stay now. I can't fit up the chimney."

LATINO "NIGHT BEFORE CHRISTMAS"

'Twas the night before Christmas and all through the casa,

Not a creature was stirring -- Caramba! Que pasa?

Los ninos were tucked away in their camas,

Some in long underwear, some in pijamas,

While hanging the stockings with mucho cuidado

In hopes that old Santa would feel obligado
To bring all children, both buenos and malos,
A nice batch of dulces and other regalos.

Outside in the yard there arose such a grito
That I jumped to my feet like a fightened cabrito.
I ran to the window and looked out afuera,
And who in the world do you think that it era?

Saint Nick in a sleigh and a big red sombrero
Came dashing along like a crazy bombero.
And pulling his sleigh instead of venados
Were eight little burros approaching volados.

I watched as they came and this quaint little hombre
Was shouting and whistling and calling by nombre:
"Ay Pancho, ay Pepe, ay Cuco, ay Beto,
Ay Chato, ay Chopo, Macuco, y Nieto!"

Then standing erect with his hands on his pecho
He flew to the top of our very own techo.
With his round little belly like a bowl of jalea,

He struggled to squeeze down our old chiminea,

Then huffing and puffing at last in our sala,

With soot smeared all over his red suit de gala,

He filled all the stockings with lovely regalos –

For none of the ninos had been very malos. Then
chuckling aloud, seeming very contento,

He turned like a flash and was gone like the viento.

And I heard him exclaim, and this is verdad,

Merry Christmas to all, and Feliz Navidad!

En la playa, un muchacha bañista dice a un mirón, "Por la forma que me mira, se ve que usted no es un caballero."   Dice su admiradór, "Y por que yo estoy viendo, se nota que usted tampoco."

> At the beach, a bathing beauty says to a "lookie-lou", "The way you're looking, I can see that you are no gentleman."
>
> Her admirer says, "And the way you're looking, I can see that you aren't, either."

"¿Qué es una selva virgen?"

"Un lugar donde la mano del hombre nunca ha puesto el pie."

> What is "virgen jungle"?
>
> A place where the hand of man has never set foot.

"¿Tu esposa te ha sido fiel?"
"Frequentemente."
>"Has your wife been faithful?"
>"Frequently."

"Mi mujer no me comprende. ¿Y la tuya?"
"No sé, nunca hablamos de ti."
>"My wife doesn't understand me. Does yours?"
>"Don't know. We never talk about you."

La maestra, algo fea, pregunta, "A ver Jaimito, la frase 'yo busco novio', ¿qué tiempo es?"
"Tiempo perdido."
>The fairly ugly teacher asks, "Let's see, Jimmy, what tense is the phrase, 'I'm looking for a boyfriend.'?"
>"A waste of time.

(Tiempo meaning both "time" and "tense")

-Pepito por qué golpeas a ese niño?
-Es que lambió mi comida.
-No, *lamio.*
-Que? También la tuya? ¡Matamos al imbecil!
>-Pepito, why'd you hit that boy?
>-Because he lickted my food.
>-No, LICKED.
>-Yours, too? Let's kill that sucker!

The pun is **lambió** (licked) and **la mio** (mine)

100

International
Mundial

Note: Google "Mexican jokes" and you'll get page after page of jokes *about* Mexicans. If you tell them to Mexicans, some will get a laugh, some will get them pissed off, some will just get blank stares since they deal with US stereotypes of Hispanics living in the US. These jokes are not *about* Mexicans, there are jokes *by* Mexicans—who can laugh at themselves and other countries as well. Some of these are biting satire on the Mexican way of life, some are aimed at other nationalities, many are simply a slapstick **Copa Mundial** of humor: Mexican selection vs. the World.

PARA QUE?

Estaba un grupo de turistas gringos recorriendo las chacras de un poblado rústico; en eso uno de ellos ve a un campesino tirado a la sombra de un árbol descansando. El gringo se le acerca y le busca conversación:

Hola amigo, ¿Cómo estar tú?

Muy bien jefe, aquí descansando.

101

Dígame, por qué usted no trabajar más por sus tierras.

¿Y para qué?

Para tener grandes cosechas y vender más.

¿Y para qué?

Así tú poder ganar más dinero y comprar ganado.

¿Y para qué?

Con el ganado hacer reproducir y vender y ganar más dinero.

¿Y para qué?

Para tener una casa bonito y vivir tranquilo y descansar.

¿Y qué estoy haciendo?

WHAT FOR?

A group of gringo tourists were touring the farms around a rustic village and came upon a peasant lying in the shade of a tree, resting. One gringo walked up to him and said:

Hello Friend, How you be?

Very good, Boss, resting here.

Tell me, why you don't work the fields more.

What for?

To have great crops and sell more.

What for?

So you can earn more money and buy livestock.

What for?

So the cattle reproduce and sell and make more money.

What for?

To have a nice home and live in peace and rest.

What am I doing?

Note: the use of infinitives in the gringo's speech is an indication of clumsy beginning Spanish.

EL INFIERNO MEXICANO

Llega un alemán al infierno y va en busca del infierno de su país, lo encuentra y le pregunta a los de la fila:

- ¿Aquí, qué te hacen?

- No pues aquí, primero te acuestan encima de una cama de clavos, luego te sientas en una silla eléctrica y al último llega el diablo y te tortura por una hora.

El alemán decepcionado va y se forma en el infierno inglés y pregunta lo mismo, a lo que le responden describiendo los mismos castigos que el infierno alemán.

Entonces se percata de una fila interminable en uno de los infiernos, por lo que se acerca y pregunta:

- ¿Qué infierno es este?

- Es el infierno mexicano

- ¿Y por qué hay tantos formados aquí?

- Lo que pasa es que aquí, los clavos se los robaron, nunca hay electricidad por falta de pago y pues el diablo llega firma y se va.

MEXICAN HELL

A German goes to hell and is given a tour of various national hells. He finds the German hell, where there are a few souls standing in line and asks:

- So what's it like?

- Well, first they lay you on a bed of nails, then sit you in an electric chair and then the devil shows up and tortures you for an hour.

Disappointed, the German goes on to the English hell, which has a similar small line, and asks the same question, to which they respond by describing the same penalties as the German hell.

At that point he spots a very long line to get into one of the hells, so he asks a damned soul:

- Which hell is this?

- The Mexican hell.

- Why are there so many in this line?

- Well, the thing is, here, the nails were all stolen, the power got cut off for non-payment and the devil just comes in, collects his pay, and takes off to the cantina.

PERROS INTELIGENTES

En una reunión internacional de pastores, tres de ellos discuten sobre cuánta inteligencia tenían y cómo la aplicaban sus respectivos perros.

El español dice:
- El perro que yo tengo es de lo más peculiar; al terminar el trabajo encierra las ovejas y les da comida, además me vigila la casa con paso marcial durante toda la noche.

El argentino dice:

- El perro que yo tengo sí que es de lo más original: al terminar el trabajo encierra a las ovejas y les da comida; vigila la casa durante toda la noche; además, lava la ropa y me blanquea la casa una vez al año.

El mexicano, con lágrimas en los ojos, replica:

- El perro que yo tenía...
- ¿Qué pasó? - preguntan los otros -
- Se murió electrocutado.
- ¿Fue por un rayo?
- No, arreglándome el televisor.

SMART DOGS

At an international shepherd's convention, three sheepherders discuss how much smart their dogs were.

The Spaniard says "My dog is really unique; after work he corrals the sheep and gives them food, then marches around the house all night to protect it."

The Argentine quickly says "My dog is even more original: after work he puts up the sheep and gives them food, then watches the house overnight, and also washes my clothes and whitewashes the house once a year."

The Mexican, with tears in his eyes, replies, "The dog I had ..." but he breaks off crying.

"What happened?" the others ask.

"He was electrocuted."

"Oh, no. Was it lightning?"

"No, he was fixing my TV."

EDÉN

En un galleria en Barcelona, Un alemán, un francés, un inglés y un mexicano comentan sobre un cuadro de Adán y Eva en el paraíso.

El alemán dice: "Miren qué perfección de cuerpos, ella esbelta y espigada, él con ese cuerpo atlético, los músculos perfilados... deben de ser alemanes."

Inmediatamente el francés reaccionó: "No lo creo, está claro el erotismo que se desprende de ambas figuras, ella tan femenina, él tan masculino, saben que pronto llegará la tentación, deben de ser franceses."

Moviendo negativamente la cabeza el inglés comenta: "Para nada, noten la serenidad de sus rostros, la delicadeza de la pose, la sobriedad del gesto, sólo pueden ser ingleses."

Después de unos segundos más de contemplación el mexicano exclama: "No estoy de acuerdo! Miren bien, no tienen ropa, no tienen zapatos, no tienen casa, sólo tienen una triste manzana para comer, no protestan y todavía piensan que están en el paraíso. ¡Esos dos sólo pueden ser mexicanos!"

PARADISE

Visting an art museum in Barcelona, a German, a Frenchman, an Englishman and a Mexican rave about a picture of Adam and Eve in paradise.

The German says, "Look how perfect are the bodies. Her, so svelte and slender, him with that athletic body and well-defined muscles... they must be Germans."

Immediately the Frenchman responded: "I do not think so. The eroticism of both figures is very clear. She is so feminine, he is so masculine; both know that temptation will soon arrive. Certainly they are French."

Shaking his head, the Englishman says: "Not at all, notice the serenity of their faces, the delicacy of pose, the sobriety of the general gesture. They can only be British."

After a few seconds of contemplation Mexican exclaims: "I disagree. Look more closely. They have no clothes, no shoes, no home, nothing to eat by a meager apple, are not allowed to complain and still think they are in paradise! Those two are Mexicans!"

MILAGRO

Un Mexicano creyente y un gringo ateo, naufragan en alta mar y cuando están a punto de morir ahogados, el Mexicano implora: "Santa Virgen de Guadalupe, envíame un flotador..."

...Y ocurre el milagro; se abren las nubes y cae un flotador a su lado, el naufrago se sube en él y se aleja .

El Gringo entiende el milagro, y también se encomienda al santo diciendo: "Santa Virgen de Guadalupe, send me a float."

Sobre una nube que baja flotando, aparece La Virgen Morena y le dice: "Lo lamento "gringuito", pero no entiendo el ingles."

MIRACLE

A Mexican believer and an atheist gringo are shipwrecked at sea and when they are about to drown, the Mexican implores: "Holy Virgin of Guadalupe, send a float ..."

And the miracle happens... the clouds open and drop a float beside the shipwrecke. The Mexican climbs up on it and paddles towards shore.

The Gringo understands the miracle, and also implores the heavens saying: "Holy Virgin of Guadalupe, send me a float."

A cloud floats lower in the heavens and the La Brown Virgin herself appears and says. "Sorry, gringo, but I don't understand English."

RECUERDOS

Se encuentran en un bar tres mercenarios: un gringo, un ingles y un Mexicano, y empiezan a presumir de sus hazañas.

Para comprobar sus aventuras, el gringo se abre la camisa, muestra en su vientre una cicatriz de 15 centímetros y dice: "New York City."

El Guatemaleco lo imita, se quita la camisa y muestra en su espalda 5 cicatrices de bala, y dice: "Guatemala City."

El Mexicano no se queda atrás, se quita los pantalones, muestra su cicatriz y dice: "Apendi-siti."

SOUVENIRS

Three mercenaries meet in a bar: a gringo, an Englishman, and a Mexican, and start to brag about their deeds.

To prove his adventures, the gringo opens his shirt, shows a 15 millimeter scar on his stomach, and says, "New York City."

The Guatemalan imitates him by taking off his shirt and showing five bullet scars on his back and saying, "Guatemala City."

The Mexican, not to be left behind, pulls off his pants, shows his scar and says, "Appendi-city."

The pun is that **appendecitis** pronounced in Spanish ends in the same sound as "city".

ARGUMENTA MEXICANA

Existen 13 pruebas de que Jesús podría haber sido mexicano:

1.- Fue condenado mientras que el verdadero ladrón fue perdonado.

2.- Cuando lo encontraron muerto estaba en paños menores.

3.- Sus familiares fueron a visitar su tumba y ya no estaba.

4.- Estaba rodeado de pobres y cada día eran más.

5.- No pagaba impuestos.

6.- Era bueno con las prostitutas.

7.- En la última cena con sus amigos no pagó la cuenta.

8.- Hizo aparecer más alcohol en una reunión donde sólo había agua.

9.- Siempre tenía una explicación para todo.

10.- Nunca tenía un peso en el bolsillo.

11.- Fue secuestrado por la policía.

12.- Fue incomunicado y torturado para que se confesara culpable.

13.- Un miembro de su banda lo delató y otro negó conocerlo.

PROOFS, MEXICAN STYLE

The evidence that Jesus could have been Mexican:

1 - He was sentenced while the real thief was forgiven.

2 - He was found dead in his underwear.

3 - His family went to visit his grave and he was gone.

4 – He was surrounded by poor and every day there were more.

5 - Did not pay taxes.

6 - He was good with prostitutes.

7 - At the last supper his friends paid the bill.

8 - He made more alcohol appear at a meeting where there was only water.

9 - He always had an explanation for everything.

10 - He ever had any money in his pocket.

11 – He was kidnapped by the police.

12 – He was held incommunicado and tortured to confess guilt.

13 - A member of his gang ratted him out and the other denied knowing him.

EL DINERO DE LOS FIELES

111

En una convención de sacerdotes se encontraba un cubano, un americano y un mexicano.

Se les aproxima una periodista y le pregunta al cubano: "Padre, ¿usted podría explicarnos qué es lo que hacen en Cuba con el dinero de los fieles?"

"Claro que sí, hija. Es muy fácil, pintamos una línea en el piso y aventamos el dinero al cielo. Lo que caiga adelante de la línea es para Dios y lo que caiga detrás de la línea es para nosotros."

"Muy bien, y ustedes los americanos, ¿qué hacen con el dinero?"

"Nosotros, marcar un círculo en el piso y lo que caer dentro del círculo ser para Dios y lo que caer afuera, ser para nosotros."

"Finalmente ustedes los mexicanos, ¿qué hacen con el dinero de los fieles?"

"Nosotros somos más justos, aventamos el dinero al cielo y lo que alcance a agarrar Dios es para él y lo demás es para nosotros."

FAITHFUL MONEY

A Cuban, an American and a Mexican were attending a convention of priests.

They were approached by a female journalist, who asked the Cuban, "Father, could you explain what they do in Cuba with the tithes of the faithful?"

"Certainly, my daughter. It's easy. We paint a line on the floor and throw money at the sky. Anything falling before the line is for God and what falls behind the line is for us."

"Very well, what do you Americans do with the money?"

"We mark a circle on the floor and what money falls within the circle goes to God and what falls outside it is for us."

"Finally, what do you Mexicans do with the money of the faithful?"

"We are more fair. We throw money at the sky and whatever God grabs is for him and the rest is for us."

LA MAQUINA

Una vez en Japón, los japoneses crearon una máquina que atrapaba ladrones. Primero la máquina la estrenaron en Japón y en menos de 30 minutos atrapó 25 ladrones.

La llevaron a Francia y en menos de 20 minutos atrapó a 17 ladrones.

La llevaron a Italia y en menos de 15 minutos atrapó a 20 ladrones.

En eso que la llevan a México y en menos de 5 minutos se robaron la máquina.

THE MACHINE

Once in Japan, the Japanese created a machine that caught thieves. First the machine debuted in Japan and in less than 30 minutes trapped 25 crooks.

113

They took it to France, where in less than 20 minutes it caught 17 thieves.

They took it to Italy and in less than 15 minutes it nailed 20 thieves.

Then they took it to Mexico, where in 5 minutes theives stole the machine.

QUINES MANDAN

Iba un buque gringo pasando por Yucatan y escuchan comunicacion de unos Yucatecos diciendoles:

Yucatecos: Aqui El Palmar 3-15 indicandoles que requerimos que desvien su rumbo 25 grados al este, cambio.

El buque gringo contesta: "Somos el U.S. 24 de la marina estadounidense, nosotros no planeamos movernos ni un grado, cambien ustedes su rumbo 15 grados oeste, cambio."

Yucatecos: "Capitan de U.S. 24, el Palmar es imposible que cambie su rumbo, por favor desvie ustedes su rumbo 25 grados este, cambio."

Gringos: (enchilados y prepotentes) "Somos el buque de un pais muy poderoso, tenemos el mas alto rango en explosivos, nos acompañan 50 hombres, 2 bombas, 8 aviones de rastreo y 5 canes entrenados, no les pedimos, LES ORDENAMOS que cambien su rumbo 15 grados al oeste, cambio."

Yucatecos: "Capitan, le habla Pepe al mando del Palmar 3-15... estamos solamente dos personas, nos acompaña unas tortas de lomo y unas cheves en la hielera, un perro y un pinche perico que esta dormido. No vamos a ningun lado, ya que les hablamos desde tierra firme por que ESTAMOS EN EL FARO EL PALMAR 3-15 asi que si no desvian su pinche barquito 25 grados al este en este mismo instante no sera nuestra culpa que se partan la madre entre las rocas porque no podemos ver cómo coño movemos nosotros el faro. Cambio…"

WHO'S IN CHARGE, HERE?

A Gringo ship off the Yucatan opened radio contact with the Mexican Navy.

Yucatecos: This is El Palmar 3-15. We require that you to deviate your course 25 degrees east, over.

The Gringo ship says, "We are the U.S. Navy vessel U.S. 24. We do not plan to move to any degree, you change your course 15 degrees west, over."

Yucatecos: "Capitan U.S. 24, it is not possible for Palmar to change its course. Please alter your course 25 degrees east, over."

Gringos: (pissed off and arrogant) "We are a captital vessel of the world's most powerful country, have the highest grade of explosives and a crew o 50 men, 2 bombers, 8 aircraft tracking missles, and 5 dogs trained to sniff narcotics. We command you to change your course 15 degrees to the west, over. "

Yucatecos: "Captain, this is Pepe in Palmar 3-15 ... we are only two people, we have some pork sandwiches and a bucket of brews in the cooler, a dog and a parrot .. which are asleep. But we are not going anywhere.

We are speaking to you from Lighthouse El Palmar, 3-15 so if you don't divert your fucking boat 25 degrees east at this moment it will not be our fault that you bust your ass on the rocks because we can not figure out how the fuck to move a lighthouse. Over..."

OFERTÓN

Una solterona se dirige al gerente de lujosa tienda, "Es verdad que hoy es la venta de empleados?"

"Si, senora mia," contesta el gerente.

"Entonces," dice la solterona, puntando el dedo y lamiendose los labios, "Llevo a ese guero de ojos azules y muchos musculotes."

BIG SALE

An old maid asked the manager of a luxury store, "Is it true that today you're having an employee sale?"

"Yes, ma-am," answered the manager.

"Then," said the old maid, pointing her figer and licking her lips "I'll take that blonde guy with the blue eyes and all the muscles."

GRINGAZO

El buen borracho hablador Miguelitros commenta a su cuate en su favorita cantina, "Ya dije, voy a veranear en Los Estados Unidos."

Su compa dice, "Por?"

Muy animada, Miquelitros explica, "Porque alla sale todo gratis. Cuando llega, un hombre te recoge en un auto del ano sin cobrar, y te trae a un restaurant bonito para comida y chupe, tampoco cobrando. Y despues a un hotel donde puedes estar todo el noche "a grapa".

No muy convencido, su cuaderno pregunta, "Y quien te conto eso?"

Con todo confianza, dice "Militros", "Bueno, Mi hermana!"

GRINGO DOINGS

The very drunk motormouth "Miquelitros" comments to his pal in his favorite bar, "I told you, I'm going to take my vacation in the United States."

His buddy asks, "Because..."

Animated, Miquelitros explains, "Because everything's free up there. When you arrive, a guy picks you up in a late model car without charging you and takes you to a nice restaurant to eat and drink, also with no charge. And afterwards to a hotel where you can stay all night for free!"

Not very convinced, his bud asks, "And who told you that?"

With total confidence, "Militros" says, "Hey, my sister!"

MUCHO SUSTO

El bebe cigüeña, llorando, pregunta a su mamá: "Mami, ¿Dónde está mi papi?"

Contesta su mamá, "Ahorita viene. Fue a hacer feliz a la esposa del pandero, llevandole un niño."

Al día siguiente, el mismo drama, pero ahora con el papá: "Papito, ¿Dónde está mi mamita querida?"

Le dice su papa, "No pasa nada, hijo." Sólo fue a llevar felicidad a una secretaria, llevandole un bebe."

A la mañana siguiente, los papás ciqüeña están preocupados porque su reteño no esta en el nido, pero en eso aparece y su mamá le contesta alivio, "Pero, ¿dónde anadabas, pequeñín?"

Riendose, el bebe cigüeña contesta, "Como ustedes, pero yo no mas llevé un susto a un universaria."

THE BIRD

A baby stork, crying, asks his mother, "Mommy, where is my daddy?"

His mother answered, "He'll be here soon. He went to make a baker's wife happy, bringing her a child."

The next day, the same drama, but now with the father stork: "Daddy, where is my dear mommy?"

His father says, "Nothing's wrong, son. She only went to bring happiness to a secretary, bringing her a baby."

The next morning, the stork parents are worried because their offspring isn't in the nest, but he shows up and his mother, relieved, asks him, "But...where did you go, little one?"

Laughing, the baby stork answers, "Like you two, but I just threw a scare into a college girl."

¿PEDINCHE O CODINCHE?

En un bar, un cuate se queja. "Me vieja siempre pidiendo. La semana pasada 300 pesos, ayer 200, hoy mil."

Su compa dice, "¡Ay, wey! ¿Que hace con tanto dinero?"

El cinico contesta, "Sepa...¡porque nunca se lo he dado!"

SPONGE OR TIGHTWAD?

In a bar, one buddy is complaining. "My old lady is always asking me for money. Last week 300 pesos, yesterday 200, today a thousand."

His pal says, "Whoa! What does she do with so much money?"

His cynical friend answers, "Who knows? I've never given her any!"

TIEMPO PARA VIRGINIDAD

Un tipo sedució una chava con mucho prisa y entusiasmo, tal que ni quitaron sus vestidos.

Despues de recubrir su aliento, dijo al muchacha, "Lo siento. Si haber sabido que era virgen, hubiera tomado mas tiempo."

Contestó ella, algo fria, "De haber sabido que tuvo mas tiempo, me huberia quitado mis pantimedias."

TIME FOR VIRGINITY

A guy seduced a chick so quickly and enthusiastically that they didn't even get undressed.

After catching his breath, he told the girl, "Sorry. If I'd known you were a virgin I'd have taken more time."

Somewhat coolly, she replied, "If I'd known you had more time, I'd have taken off my pantyhose."

MALA SUERTE

Al dirigirse a casa, Paco Tilla es bajado de su auto por unos judiciales, quienes le pega y, sin decir agua va, se llevan su coche y se van. Para colmo, es atacado por unos cacos que le roban de todo y de paso, lo dejan atado a un poste, doblado.

El pobre pasa ahí todo la noche, hasta que, al amancer, pasa un tipo fortalón, que dice, "¿Que le paso, mi buen?"

Contesta Paco, "Es que anoche unos judas se llevaron mi auto. Luego me asaltaron unos cacos y me dejaron asi. ¡Uff, ayer no fu me día!"

"Y creo," dice el fortalchon, bajando los chones del imobilizado Paco, "¡Que hoy tampoco!"

TOUGH LUCK

Driving home, Paco Tilla is taken out of his car by Judicial Police, who hit him and, without saying what for, take his car and drive off. To top it off, he's attacked by some muggers who rob him of everything and take off leaving him tied up to a lamp post, bent over with hands tied to his ankles.

The poor guy spends the night there until, at daybreak, a muscular guy comes by and says, "What happened to you, my good man?"

122

Paco answers, "Last night some judicials took my car, then some muggers robbed me and left me like this. Wow, yesterday just wasn't my day!"

"I got a feeling," says the big guy, pulling down Paco's underpants, "That today isn't either!"

DE PELOS

Una muchacha presenta su hijo a su madrina, quien dice, "¡Pero miro nomás que preciosidad de esquincle!"

Dando un abrazo al plebe, dice, "¡Y qué bonito pelito! ¿Asi lo tiene su papa, m'ijita?"

"¿Pos quien sabe, madrinita?" contesta la muchacha, "¡Porque el muy desgraciado ni el sombrero se quitó!"

HAIRY STORY

A girl introduces her son to her godmother, who says, "Just look what a precious kiddo!"

Hugging the kid, she says, "And what pretty hair! Is his father's like that, hon?"

"Beats me, godmother," answers the girl, "The asshole never took off his hat."

MEJOR

Acostada en el divan, la preciosa chava le cuenta su problema al psiquíatra.

123

"Tengo el carácter tan debil," dice, "Que los hombres consiquen de mí lo que quieren."

Quitandose una lagrima, sigue con, "Y luego me entran remodimientos de conciencia."

El loquero dice serio, "Bueno, hay various métodos para reforzar el carácter."

"¡Ay no!" dice la muchacha, "Lo que yo quiero es que desparezcan los remordimientos."

BETTER YET

Lying on the couch, the cute chick tells her problem to the psychiatrist.

"I've got such weak character," she says, "That men get whatever they want off me."

Wiping a tear, she continues, "And then I get regrets."

Seriously, the shrink says, "Okay, there are several ways we can strengthen your character."

"Oh no!" says the girl, "What I want is to get rid of the regrets!"

CEGATÓN

Un conejo silvestre llama un zorro, "Magu". Su compa pregunta por qué y contesta, "Porque está re ciego el condenado¡El otro dia le queria hacer el amor a un pedo!"

BLIND DATE

A wild rabbit calls a skunk "Magoo". His buddy asks why and he answers, "Because the poor guy is so blind that the other day he tried to make love to a fart!"

PROGNOSTICO

Como las ventas de la companía rompen todos los récords, el dueño dice sarcástico a su chamorruda secretaria, "¿Ya ve, Normita? Se imagina lo que usted tendria ahora se me hubiera concedido lo que hace algun tiempo le pedí?"

Iqual de sarcástica contesta la secre, "Si Señor. ¡Siete meses de embarazo!"

FORECAST

With the company breaking all sales records, the owner mentions sarcastically to his "thighsable" secretary, "Now you see, Norma? Imagine where you'd be now if you'd just come across with what I wanted that time?"

"Sure, boss," the secretary replied. equally sarcastic, "Seven months pregnant!"

POR SÍ LAS DUDAS

La maestra pone como exámen de ortografía, escribir la fábula de "La Gallina de los Huevos de Oro". Dice, "Los que hayan terminado, pueden irse."

A la salida, Luisita pregunta a Pepito, "Oye ¿Huevos se escribe con 'V' chica o 'B' grande?"

"No se, " contesta el escuincle, "Y pa' evitar problemas, mejor escribí, 'Cojones'."

WHEN IN DOUBT

For the spelling test, the teacher assigns writing the fable of "The Goose that Laid the Golden Eggs". She says, "Those who have finished may leave."

At the exit, Luisita asks Pepito, "Hey, do you spell 'huevos' with a 'v' or 'b'?"

"I don't know," replies the brat, "So to avoid problems, I just wrote 'cojones'."

(Note the use of "**chica**" and "**grande**"--the only way to distinguish "v" and "b" in Spanish, since they are pronounced the same.)

TU CU

Nopalita fue a una casa a pedir chamba y dijo al amo, "Tonces qué, siñor, ¿'Aste', no me va a dar trabajo de sirvienta?"

El duéno dijo, "Primero me tienes que enseñar tu curriculum."

Ensenandole el dedo, Nopalita gritó, "¡Mangos que! Por eso no me he casado, para no enseñar nada."

RESUMÉ

Nopalita went to a house to ask for work and said to the man of the house, "What you think, Meester? Won't you hire me as a servant?"

The owner said, "First show me your curriculum."

Showing him the finger, Nopalito yelled, "Screw that! If I showed that to everybody I'd be married."

She's confusing "**curriculum**" because it starts with the same syllable as "**culo**" or "**cucu**" Note the "**siñor**". Indicating a hick accent--calling the girl Nopalita after nopales is another hick clue. Hillbillies often turn the "e" to "i", saying things like "**no li hace**." The '**aste**' for "**usted**" is another backwoods tag.

OCUPADÓN

Un indocumentado Mexicano trataba de regulizar su situación en los Estados Unidos, y el funcionario de migración le dice: "¿Tu apreciar lo qué vale vivir en este pais?"

Contesta que sí y del escritorio pregunta, "¿Y tu saber que aquí todous somous iquales?"

Y, "Sí."

Sique el funcionario, "A ver. ¿Podrias ser tu, presidente de los Estadous Unidous?"

Dice, "No," y el otro pregunta, "¿Por que no?"

"Porque tengo mucha camba en la taqueria."

BOOKED UP

An undocumented Mexican worker was trying to get resident status in the United States, and the official asks him, "You appreciate what it's worth, living in this country?"

He says yes and the guy at the desk asks, "And know that here we all be equal?"

"Yes", so the official continues, "Let's see. Could you be president of the United States?"

He says, "No," and the other asks, "Why not?"

"Because I've got a lot of work at the taco shop."

ENTREVISTA

Don Teofilo Telaraña recibe la visita de una reportera que lo quiere entrevistar. Dice ella, "Dicen que pertenece usted a una familia ilustre."

"Sí," dice el ruco, "Por parte de padre desciendo de Hamoroso Diacá y de Tercieto Diallá. Por parte de me madre, provengo de los Mariquez y Cuellar, y el Duque Canocan. Cuento enre mis antpasados al Marques Copelais."

Impresionada, la muchacha exclama, "¡Caramba! Que pedigrí se carga."

Muy ofendido, responde, "De ninguna manera, Señorita. Le asequro que estoy sobrio."

INTERVIEW

Don Teofilo Telaraña gets a visit from a reporter who wants to interview him. She says, "They say that you belong to an illustrious family."

"Yes," the old guy says, "On my father's side I'm descended from Hamoroso Diaca and Tercieto Dialla. On my mother's side I come from the Manriquez y Cuellar, and the Duke of Canocan. The Marquis Copelais is my ancestor."

Impressed, the girl exclaims, "Wow! What a pedigree you've got."

Offended, he says, "By no means, Miss. I assure you I'm sober."

Pedigri resembles **pedo**: literally "fart", but also a crude term for "drunk"

129

SE BUSCA

El viejo cliente del Banco pregunta curioso al gerente, "Oiga, supe que andaban buscando a un cajero."

"Asi es."

"¿Y como está eso?" pregunta, "Si apenas la semana pasada contrataron a un cajero."

"Pues sí," contesta el gerente, "¡Precisamente a ése andamos buscando."

WANTED

Curious, an old customer asked the bank manager, "Hey, I hear you're looking for a teller."

"That's right."

"And how's that?" he asks, "You just hired a teller last week."

"Well, yeah," says the manager, "That's exactly the guy we're looking for!"

REBANE

En su primer día de trabajo, "El Ñoño" sale temprano de la fábrica de embutidos y al salir, lo detiene el vigilante. "¿A dónde va, jovencito?"

"Me voy," dice, "Me despideron porque metí el dedo a una rebanadora."

"¡Achis!" dice el vigilante, "Déjeme ver su dedo." Y mirandolo, dice, "Oiga, si no tiene nada."

"¡Pues claro!" dice el recien despedido, "Porque era una rebanadora de jamón y ¡ A ella también la corrieron!"

A SLICE

His first day at work at the meat factory, "El Ñoño" is leaving early and the watchman stops him, "Where you going, youngster?"

"I'm leaving," he says, "They fired me because I stuck my finger in a slicer."

"Ouch!" says the watchman, "Let me see your finger." Looking at it, he says, "Listen, there's nothing wrong with it."

"Well, sure," says the recent firee, "Because I'm talking about a ham slicer, and they fired her, too."

PERDIDA

La oxigenada "La Coyota" le dice a su esculptural compa, "La Pelos de Elote", "Oye, mana ¿Sabias que la vanidosa de "La Curvas" esta perdiendo su belleza?"

Contesta la nena, "Estás mal informada, Loca, no la perdió....¡La vendió!"

LOST

The busty La Coyota says to her sculptured buddy, Pelos de Elote, "Hey, Sis, did you know that vain bitch La Curvas is losing her looks?"

The chick replies, "You're misinformed, you nut. She's not losing them, she's selling them!"

SEÑALES

Al pasar una revolcable muchachona en la calle, dice "La Pelos" a "La Curvas", "Mira, ahi va 'La Semáforo."

"Por qué le apodan así, manita?"

"Porque despues de las doce en la noche, ¡Ningún chavo la respeta!"

SIGNALS

Passing a "turnoverable" babe in the street, "La Pelos" says to "La Curvas", "Look, there goes 'Miss Stoplight'."

"Why'd they nickname her that?"

"Because after midnight, none of the boys respect her."

INCULTA

Un joven decente, culto, y bien educado invita a salir as su descocada y inculta pero buenona vecinita y al final de la cita, el cuate dice, "Fíjate que estaré lejos un año, voy a estudiar en el extranjero, y quisiera pedirte, si...¿Aceptas tener conmigo una relacion epistolar?"

Dice la vecina, "¡Claro que sí! No mas dime, ¿Vamos a algún lugar o nos pasamos al asiento de atras?"

UNEDUCATED

A decent, educated, and well-brought-up young man takes out his brainless and uneducated, but very sexy, neighbor and at the end of the date, the guy asks, "Look, I'm going to be far away for a year, I'm going to study abroad and I'd like to ask you if you would like to have a penpal relationship with me."

The "girl next door" says, "Of course! Just tell me, are we going somewhere or just getting in the back seat?"

NIÑERA

Una señora recibe un telefonazo de una de sus tantas amigas, invitandola a una despida de soltera.

"Hijoles, hoy no puedo," dice, "Mi sirvienta salió y tengo que cuidar a mis hijos y esposo."

Una semana despues, vuelve a recibír otra invitación
de la misma amiga pero dice, "Tampoco puedo hoy.
Mis hijos se van a un campamiento y tengo que
quedarme a cuidar a mi marido y a la sirvienta."

BABYSITTER

A lady gets a phone call from one of her many friends,
inviting her to a bachelorette party.

"Gee, I can't today," she says, "My maid is off and I
have to look after my kids and husband."

A week later, she gets another invitation from the same
friend and says, "I can't today, either. My kids went to
camp and I have to stay here to look after my husband
and the maid."

NO ES LO MISMO

"La Curvas" quiera que todas las gringas que estudian
español sabían qué no es lo mismo "un metro de
encaje negro" que "Negro, encájame un metro".

"La Curvas" wants all the gringas who study Spanish
to know that there is a difference between "a meter of
black lace" and "Negro, put a meter in my box".

Y que tampoco es lo mismo, tu novia pisó un clavo
que me clavo a tu novia en el piso.

And also that, "Your girlfriend stepped on a nail" isn't
the same as "I nailed your girlfriend on the floor."

(**Piso** is both the noun "floor" and verb "step".)

CURIOSITA

Paquita y su mamá se ponen el traje de baño en el
vestidor de damas. La niña echa un vistazo alrededor
y curiosa pregunta:

"Oye, mami ¿Por qué las mujeres tenemos esto
abajito?"

"Ay hijita." responde la señora suspirando, "Porque si
lo tuviéramos atrás... ¡seriamos alcancías!"

CURIOUS

Paquita and her mom are trying on bathing suits in the
ladies dressing room. The little girl took a look around

and curiously asked, "Hey, mom, why do we women have that down there?"

"Well honey," her mom whispers, "Because if we had it in back, we'd be piggy banks."

ABUSADILLA

Acudiendo a la residencia donde solicitan una familia la buenérrima trenzudita es entrevistada por la doña:

"Y dime muchacha, ¿Sabes servir una mesa para varios invitados?"

"Pos si, siñora. Sé servir de las dos formas."

"¿Cuales dos formas, muchacha?" pregunta intrigada la dueña de la casa.

"Pos...¡Pa' que vuelvan y pa' que no vuelvan, siñora!"

MAID TO ORDER

Applying at the residence where the family had advertised for help, the cute little "braid head" is interviewed by the lady of the house.

"Tell me, Miss, do you know how to serve a table for several guests?"

"Duh, yeah, Mum," I know how to serve both ways."

"What do you mean, 'Both ways?" asked the house owner, intrigued.

"Well...so they'll come back and so they won't."

Calling a girl trenzuda or Trenzitas means she wears her hair in long braids: in other words she is an "**Indita**" and therefore ignorant and backward.

DE TODOS MODOS

Casi al final de la pachanga, la ñora acerca a su marido que ya anda hasta el cepillo y ni en cuenta de lo que ocurre a su alrededor.

"¿Nos vamos, querido?"

"¡Hip! ¿Queeeeeeeé?" le contesta.

"Que si ya nos vamos a la cama," dice su calienta mujer.

"Como no, preshiosha." contesta el borrachín, "De todos modos mi vieja me pegará cuando llegue a la casha a esta hora."

ANYWAY

Almost at the end of the party, the young matron approaches her husband, who is so bombed he doesn't know what's going on, and says, "Shall we go, dear?"

"Hic, huuuuh?" he replies.

"Let's go to bed," says his horny wife.

"Why not, cutie," the drunk answers, "My wife's gonna slug me anyway for getting home this late."

¿PARA QUÉ?

El nervioso novio llega a pedir la mano de su galana a su gigante y feróz papá, deciendo, "Soy paraguayo y quiero casarme con su hija pa' follar a gusto."

El papá contesta enojado, "¿Para que?"

Suavemente dice el muchacho, "Paraquayo."

FOR WHAT?

The nervous boyfriend comes to ask for the hand of his sweetheart from her huge, ferocious dad and says, "I'm from Paraguay and I want to marry your daughter so I can screw her but good."

The dad angrily asks, "For WHAT?"

Smoothly the kid says, "Paraguay."

¡YA QUE INSISTE!

Cuando subian al piso sesenta neuve del Empire States en Nueva York, el ascensor falla, el turista Mexicano se asoma y al ver que los cables se rompen, dice apurado a la gringocha:

"¡Nos quedan como quince minutos de vida, máximo!"

Ella, sin pensar, levanta su falda y le dice, "¡Plis, hazme sentir mujer!"

El tipo, quitandose los pantalones, le dice "Pues, plánchalos!"

IF YOU INSIST

When the elevator breaks at floor sixty nine of the Empire State Building the Mexican tourist looks up, sees the broken cables, and blurts to the gringa in the car, "We've got fifteen minutes to live, tops!"

Without thinking she pulls up her skirt and says, "Please, make me feel like a woman!"

The guy takes off his pants and says, "Here, iron these!"

LA MISMA

Dos bribones, Carlitros y Huesalitros, salen de su oficina-bar Las Americas, bien pedos y charlando sobre la familia. Comenta Carlitros, "Pues yo tengo once hijos, mi Huesalitros."

Dice el otro, "¡Achis! ¿Y con la misma?"

Contesta su cuate, "Claro, wey...pero con diferentes mujeres, que pa' eso so macho."

SAME ONE

Two lushes, Carlitros and Huesalitros, are leaving their office/bar Las Americas, shitfaced and talking about family matters. Carlitros says, "Hey, I've got eleven kids, my Huesalitros."

The other says, "Wow! All with the same one?"

His pal answers, "Of course, dummy...but with different women, that's why I'm macho."

COSITA

El recién casado pregunta a su más que buenisima mujer: "Oye, mi reina adorada, ¿Aun conservas tu virginidad?"

Contesta la chava, dejandose caer su bata, "Claro que no, mi amor. Pero aqui está el estuchito en que venia."

THINGIE

The newlywed asks his more than gorgeous wife, "Listen, my adored queen, do you still have your virginity?"

The babe answers, letting her robe fall away, "Of course not, my love. But here's the case it came in."

DERECHOS

Una muchacha muy bien formada, y con vestida casi insuficiente, pretendió entrar al Basílica de San Pedro, pero el guardia suizo le niega.

Ella protesta, "Pero si tengo el derecho divino."

Contesta el guardia, "Y el izquierdo también, pero con tamaño escote no puede entrar."

141

RIGHT NICE

A very well-built, scantily clad young woman tried to enter Saint Peter's Basilica, but the Swiss Guard wouldn't let her come in.

The young lady protested prettily, "But don't I have a divine right?"

The guard answered, "Yes, and a nice left, too. But with that much cleavage showing, you don't get in."

REGALO

Un joven quería comprarle un regalo a su novia para su cumpleaños. Como se habían hecho novios hacia muy poco, lo pensó mucho y decidió que un par de guantes sera muy bien regalo, sería un poco romántico, sin ser muy personal.

La hermana de la novia lo acompañó a la tienda a escoger los guantes y compro unos blancos. La hermana aprovechó que estaba en el centro comercial y compró unas pantaletas que necesitaba. Cuando envuelve el regalo, la vendadora se equivocó y envolvió las pantaletas en vez de los guantes.

Sin revisar el contendido del paquete el joven envió el regalo a su novia con la siguiente nota:

Escogí este regalo porque he notado que no usas cuando salimos por la noche; si no hubiera por tu hermana hubiera escogido los largos con botones, pero ella se probó estos cortos que son más fáciles de quitar.

Quería excoger una tonalidad mas delicada, pero la vendedora me mostró los que ella usa; no se los había cambiado en tres semanas y no se la nota para nada de mugre. Le pedí a la vendadora que se probara estos que compre para ti y se veían muy bien.

Quisiera estar contigo para ponérles por primera vez; no tengo duda que otras manos los tocaran antes de que te vuelva a ver. Cuando te los quites, recuerda soplarlos antes de guardarlos pues es natural que cojan un poquito de humedad.

Pienso no más en cuantas veces los voy a besar; espero que los uses para mi, el próximo viernes por la noche.Recibe todo mi amor.

P.D. La última moda es usarlos doblándos un poquito hacia abajo, para que se vea el peluche.

THE GIFT

A young man wanted to buy his girlfriend a present for her birthday. Since they had been sweethearts a short time, he thought about it a lot and decided that a pair of gloves would be a good gift, a little romantic without being too personal.

The girlfriend's sister went with him to the store to pick out the gloves and he bought a pair of white ones. The sister took advantage of being in the shopping center to buy a pair of panties that she needed. When she wrapped the present, the salesgirl made a mistake and wrapped the panties instead of the gloves.

Without checking the contents of the package, the boyfriend send the present with the following note: I chose this present because I have noticed that you don't wear any when we go out at night; if it hadn't been for your sister I'd have gotten the big kind with buttons, but she showed me how these short ones are easier to take off.

I would have gotten a darker color, but the salesgirl showed me hers; she's been wearing them for three weeks and they don't show any dirt. I asked her to model these for me and they looked very good on her.

I wish I could be with you the first time you put these on, I have no doubt that other hands will touch them before I see them again. When you take them off, be sure to blow in them before putting them away, since its natural that they will get moist inside from use.

I think only of how many times I will kiss them; I hope you will wear them for me next Friday night. All my love.

P.S. The latest fashion is to wear them turned down to show off the fuzzy stuff inside.

CONFUNDIDA

El galan ha servido unas tequilas a la muchacha muy bonita y mucho mas joven y crea que ha llegado al cumbre de su seducción al sentarse con ella en su cama.

Palmando la ahomada, dice, "Bueno, guerida, nadamas pongas tu linda cabecita aqui para descansar y deliciar."

Ella, un poco ebrio y insegura de la situación, dice, "Ay, Señor, no confunda."

El contesta suavemente, "No hay problema, chulis. Quitamos la funda."

CONFUSION

The playboy had served a few tequilas to the pretty and much younger girl and thought that he'd arrived at the peak of his seduction when she sat down with him on his bed.

Patting the pillow, he says, "Well, dear, just put your pretty little head here to rest and enjoy."

A little drunk and unsure of the situation, she says, "Whoa, Mister, don't confuse me."

He smoothly replies, "No problem, cutie. We'll take off the pillowcase."

The play is between **confunda**, meaning "confuse" and **con funda**, meaning "with the case."

COMPREHENSION MASCULINO

Un hombre va conduciendo por la carretera cuando de pronto ve que en dirección contraria viene una mujer conduciendo su auto como loca y que al acercarse, baja el vidrio y le grita:

¡PUEEEEEEEEEERCOOOOOOOOOO!

El hombre que obviamente no se pudo quedar callado, baja su vidrio y le grita:
¡MUUUUUUUUUULAAAAAAAA!

En eso, al doblar la curva, ¡pum! se estrella con un gran puerco que estaba en medio de su carril.

MALE UNDERSTANDING

A man was driving on the highway when suddenly he sees a woman coming in the opposite direction, driving her car like crazy and who on approaching lowers her window and yells at him "PIIIIIIIIG!

The man obviously couldn't stay silent, lowers his window and yells to her: MUUUUULE!

At that, upon rounding the curve, Bang! He crashes into a big pig in the middle of his lane.

ASOMBROSO

Doña Reumas que buscaba a su ruco marido Don Telaraño, entra al cuarto de la chacha y le ve haciendo el mero cuchi-cuchi con la sexi servienta. Sorprendida, ella exclama, "¡Madre de Dios!

No te crei capaz de hacer semejante cosa."

Contesta orgulloso el rucalin, "¡Y dos veces, viejita!"

AWESOME

Lady Reumas, looking for her old husband Don Telaraño, enters the maid's room and sees him doing the fucky-fucky with the sexy servant. Amazed, she exclaims, "Mother of God! I didn't think you capable of doing such a thing."

Proudly, the old fart answers, "And twice, honey!"

EMBUSCADA

Cierta tarde que Caperucita Roja caminaba por el bosque se le aparece el lobo, diciendo,"Ven Caperuza, vamos tras los arbustos, quiero hacerte una proposición endecorosa."

"No, lobo, " contesta la jovencita, "No iré."

"¿Por qué, Caperuza?" siga el lobo, "Andale, no seas rejega."

"No, a mi mami no le gustaria."

"¿Como no?" dice el lobo, "A tu mamá, le rete encantó."

AM-BUSH

A certain afternoon, Little Red Riding Hood was walking in the forest and the wolf appeared, saying, "Come on, Hoodlet, let's go behind those bushes. I want to give you an indecent proposal."

"No wolf," answered the young thing, "I won't go."

"Why not, Red?" the wolf kept on, "Come on, don't be a prude."

"No, my mom wouldn't like it."

"Actually," said the wolf, "Your mom totally loved it."

HABANEROS

Dos prisioneros cubanos charlan. Dice uno, "Así ue...¿Cuantos años te dieron?"

Contesta el otro, "Diez, mi negro José."

"Y que hiciste?"

"¡Nada!"

"¡Mentiroso!" grita José, "Por no hacer nada, solo condenan a cinco años."

HAVANANS

Two Cuban prisoners are chatting. One says, "Well, how many years did they give you?"

The other answers, "Ten, my man Jose."

"And what did you do?"

"Nothing!"

"Liar!" shouts Jose, "For doing nothing they only give you five years."

PREVENIDO

Un campesino está dando mantenimiento a su burro, cuando llega su compadre y dice, "Oye ¿Y pa' qué engrasas al asno?"

Dice el primero, "Es que lo voy a vender."

"Y cuanto vas a pedir?"

"Diez mil pesos," dice el dueño.

148

"¡Ufta!" dice su vecino, "Pos te van a decir que te lo meta por el trasero."

"¡Por eso lo estoy engrasando!"

PREVENTION

A farmer is doing a little maintenance on his burro when his friend comes up and says, "Hey, why are you greasing the jackass?"

The first farmer says, "Because I'm selling it."

"How much you going to ask?"

"Ten thousand pesos," says the owner.

"Oof!" says his neighbor, "They're going to tell you to stick it up your butt."

"That's why I'm greasing it."

SOSPECHAS

Un ranchero llega a casa de su compadre. El anfitrión dice, "Pásale, compadre. ¿Y la comadre? ¿No que también iba a venir?"

"Pos, no pudo," dice el envitado, "La he dejado con quarenta en cama."

"Caray, compadre, lo siento," dice su compa, "Ya lo dice el dicho, 'La que nace pa' puta, jamas lo oculta."

SUSPICIONS

A rancher goes to his friend's house. The host says, "Come in, partner. And your wife? Isn't she going to come, too?"

"Aww, she couldn't," says the guest, "I left her in bed with forty."

"Whoa, pal, I'm sorry." says his buddy, "Like the saying goes, "When they're born to be a whore, it always shows."

"With forty" refers to a temperature of 40 degrees, centigrade, a serious fever.

PORQUERÍA

Un campesino regresa del mercado a su pueblo con un cochino que acaba de comprar. Su compadre pregunta, "Oye, compa, ¿asi que es muy chiquito tu despacho, donde vas a poner ese puerco?"

"Pos, bajo la cama," contesta.

"¿Y el olor y la pesta?"

"Tendrá que acostumbrarselo."

PIGSTY

A farmer comes back from market with a pig he just bought. His buddy asks, "Hey, pal, since your place is so small, where are you going to put that porker?"

"Well, under the bed," he answers.

"What about the smell and the flies?"

"He'll just have to get used to it."

REGLAS DE LA ETIQUETA

En la suite nupcial entre rechinados de colchón y jadeos, se eschucha una quejosa voz, "¡Jaime! Si fureras una caballero, no me obligarias hacer ésto."

Y un voz varonil contestando, "¡Cállate Pilar! Que si fueras una dama...¡No hablarías con la boca llena!

RULES OF ETIQUETTE

In the bridal suite, amidst squeaks from the mattress and panting, can be heard a complaining voice, "Jaime! If you were a gentleman you wouldn't make me do this."

And a male voice replying, "Shut up, Pilar! If you were a lady you wouldn't talk with your mouth full."

VIOLADA DE NUEVA

La curvosa muchacha despierta llorando su esposo, poco joven. "¡Buaaaa...me violaron!" grita, "Creí que eras tú, hasta que empezo el segundo!"

RAPED AGAIN

The curvaceous girl woke up her not-so-young husband, crying. "Waaahhhh....I've been raped!" she cried, "I thought it was you, until he started to do it the second time."

ETERNO

"La Defensas" suspira romanticamente, al preguntar a la rechupeteable "La Curvas", "Manita, ¿Tú crees en el amor eterno?"

"Claro que creo en el!" contesta su amiga, "Yo he tenido doce ó trece de ésos."

ETERNAL

Sighing romantically, "La Defensas" asks the extremely "nibbleable" "La Curvas", "Honey, do you believe in eternal love?"

"Of course I believe in it!" replies her buddy, "I've had twelve or thirteen of them."

CONQUISTA

Reunidos a la mesa, a la hora de la cena, Pepito pregunta, "Oye, jefe, ¿Es verdad que al hombre sel conquista por el estómago?"

"Es verdad, Pepito." contesta su papá, "Yo me casé con tu madre en cuanto le empezó a crecer el suyo."

CONQUEST

Together at the table at supper hour, Pepito asks, "Hey, 'Boss', is it true that a man is conquered by the stomach?"

"It's true, Pepito," his dad answers, "I married your mother when hers started to swell."

MACHOTE

El machotista señor llega a su casa y encuentra a su hijo tejiendo un púlover. Enojado, dice, "Raphael, ¿otra vez jugando con eso? ¿Por qué no haces cosas de niños?"

"Ésto es de niño, papi, "dice el chico, "¿No ves que el estambre es azul?"

MACHO MAN

The very "macho" guy comes home and finds his son knitting a pullover. Angry, he says, "Raphael, are you playing that again? Why can't you do boy's things?"

"This is a boy's thing, daddy," says the kid, "Can't you see the yarn is blue?"

LAS RUBIAS

¿Cual es la differencia entre una rubia y una papa?
Que la papa siempre es cultivada

¿Cual es la differencia entre una rubia y un mosquito?
Que cuando le pegas al mosquito, deja de chupar.

¿Cual es la differencia entre una rubia y un perro?
El precio del collar

¿Cual es la differencia entre una rubia y una bola de boliche?
Que en una bola de boliche sólo puedes meter tres dedos

¿Cual es la differencia entre una rubia frigida y la gelatina?
Que la gelatina se mueve cuando la comes

BLONDES

What's the difference between a blonde and a potato?
Potatoes are cultivated

What's the difference between a blonde and a mosquito?
When you hit a mosquito it stops sucking

What's the difference between a blonde and a dog?
The price of the collar (necklace).

What's the difference between a blonde and a bowling ball?
You can only stick three fingers into a bowling ball

TAMAÑO

Un tipo entra una tienda del barrio acompañado de dos monumentales pero corrientones cueros y dice...

"Dos pepsis, por favor."

Lo de la tienda pregunta, "¿Familiares?"

"No, son putas," dice el wey, "Pero tienen sed."

QUESTION OF SIZE

A guy comes into a corner store with two "monumental", but coarse "bods, and says, "Two Pepsis, please."

The clerk asks, "Family?"

"No, they're 'ho's," the guy says, "But they're thirsty."

When the clerk says **familiar**, he's asking if he wants the large family sized Pepsis, not if the women are family members.

DESVELADA

Despues de tres colchonazos en su noche de estreno, los recien casados descansan un poco, respirando profundamente. El esposo recien probado tiene sueños, y dice a su flamante esposa, "¿No vas a dormir?"

"No," contesta, "Mi mami dijo que esta noche tendria una experiencia inolvidable y no me la quiero perder."

WIDE AWAKE

After three "mattress attacks" on their "opening night", the newly weds rest a little, breathing deeply. The recently proven husband is sleepy and says to his spanking new wife, "Aren't you going to sleep?"

"No," she replies, "My mommy told me that tonight I'd have an unforgettable experience and I don't want to miss it."

SALVAJE

En la tienda de mascotas, un tipo pregunta, "¿No tiene patos salvajes?"

"No," dicen el vendedor, "Pero si quiere le encabrono una gallina."

WILD

In a pet store, a guy asks, "Don't you have wild ducks?"

"No," says the salesman, "But if you want, I can piss off a chicken."

Salvaje means both "wild" as "undomesticated" and "savage".

DE HUEVO

El peluquero pregunta al cliente, "¿Desea el champú al huevo?"

"No", dice fuerte el tipo, "¡A la cabeza!"

EGG NOGGIN

The barber asks a customer, "Would you like egg shampoo?"

"NO," the guy says, forcefully, "On my head!"

The usual play between "eggs" and "balls", based here on "egg shampoo".

Cuando una alemana dice "ya" es que "sí". Y cuando una mexicana dice "sí" es que"ya".

> When a German girl says "Jah", it means "yes". And when a Mexican girl says "yes", it means "right now".

LA BICICLETA

Dos estudiantes de ingeniería se encuentan en el campus y uno dijo al otro: "¿De donde sacaste esa magnifica bicicleta?"

El segundo contestó: "Bueno, yo estaba caminando por ahí ayer, pensando en mis trabajos, cuando una hermosa mujer apareció sobre esta bicicleta. Tiró la bicicleta al suelo, se sacó toda su ropa y dijo: "Toma lo que quieras."

El primer ingeniero estuvo de acuerdo: "¡Buena elección! La ropa probablemente no te hubiera quedado."

THE BICYCLE

Two engineering students met on campus and one said to the other, "Where did you get that great bicycle?"

The other answered, "Well, I was walking her yesterday, thinking about my work, when a beautiful woman appeared on this bike. She threw the bike on the ground, tore off all her clothes, and said, "Take whatever you like."

The first engineer agreed, "Good choice! The clothes probably wouldn't have fit you."

MAMA MILLA

Dos Argentinos miran el tele, donde anuncian carrera de motos, la "Baja 1000".

Dice uno, "Epa, mil millas en un moto? Que barbaro, che.

El otro pregunta "¿Dime, che, cuanto mide la milla?"

Contesta su amigo, "La mia, 10 pulgadas; la tuya no se."

MEASURING UP

Two Argentines watching TV where there's an ad for the motorcycle race, "Baja 1000."

One says, "Hey, a thousand miles on a motorcycle? Awful, buddy."

The other asks, "Tell me, pal, How long's a mile?"

His friend answers, "Mine'sa 10 inches. Yours, I don't know."

The pun **milla/mia** works best using the "high class" pronunciation of "ll"--kind of like "zh"...see pronunciation guide at back of book. And with an Argentine accent, which is basically the same as our idea of an Italian accent.

"**Che**" is widely used by Argentines as an address, like saying, "Hey, man or "What's up, bro?" Argentines are often called "**che**" in other countries, like calling somebody "Tex". Very similar to the use of **ese** by Latinos in the USA--and in fact, both words really mean "that", as in "that guy."

¡QUÉ BÁRBARO!

Mientras aguardaba turno en la barbería, un cliente vió que el hombre al que estaban afeitando en el sillón recibía una leve cortadura. La segunda vez que esto ocurrió, el cliente se tocó la herida, se miró el dedo manchado de sangre y luego le preguntó al peluquero:
— ¿Tiene guardada por ahí otra razura?
—Si. ¿Por qué?
— Es que me gustaría defenderme.

BARBER-ITY

While awaiting his turn in the barber shop, a customer saw that the man who was being shaved in the chair received a slight cut. The second time this happened, the customer touched the wound. The customer looked at the blood-stained finger and then asked the barber, "Do you have another razor?"

--Yes, why?

--Because I'd like to defend myself.

Note that "barber" is translated here as the Spanish sytle **barberia** and the Mexican **peluquero**.

MEMORABLE

Una pareja de ancianos llegó a un restaurante. El mesero quedó impresionado al ver que el viejecito se dirigía a su mujer con palabras muy melosas: Ven, mi vida... Siéntate, mi cielo... ¿Qué vas a comer, reina?... El empleado no pudo con la curiosidad y, aprovechando un momento en que ella fue al baño, preguntó al anciano:

— Perdone, Señor. ¿Cuánto llevan de casados?

— Sesenta y cinco años.

— ¡Lo felicito de veras! — exclamó el mesero — No es normal hablar con esa ternura a la esposa después de tanto tiempo.

Es que ya no recuerdo cómo se llama — confesó el viejecito.

MEMORABLE

An old couple arrived at a restaurant. The waiter was impressed to see that the old man directed very sweet words at his wife: Come, my love… Have a seat, my heaven… What are you going to have, my queen? Curious, the waiter took advantage of a moment when she went to the bathroom, and asked the old guy:

--Pardon the liberty,sir, but how long have you been married?

--Seventy five years.

--I really congratulate you! exclaimed the waiter. It's not normal to speak so tenderly to one's wife after such a long time.

--It's because I don't remember her name, answered the old gent.

ALIVIADO

El dueño de la fábrica de detergentes dice feliz a su contador, "Fijate que mi secretaria me acaba de decir que nuestra detergente is tan suave que ella lo usa para bañarse sus partes privadas."

"Gracios a Dios, jefe," exclama aliviado su empleado, "Cuando entré después de que salió su secretaria pensé que usted tenia rabia."

The owner of a detergent factory happily said to his accountant, "Check it out, my secretary just told me that our detergent is so soft she uses it to wash her private parts."

"Thank God, boss," exclaimed the relieved employee. "When I came in after she left, I thought you had rabies."

LABOR FORCE

El mismo jefe, padre industrial, dice a su pequeño hijo, "Ya sé que de regalo de Navidad querías una hermanita, pero no hay tiempo."

Pregunta el niño, "¿Ni poniendo más hombres a trabajar?"

That same boss, a job-oriented dad, says to his little son, "I know you want a little sister for Christmas, but there's no time."

The kid asks, "Not even putting more men on the job?"

JAPONES EN ESPAÑOL

Como se dice en Japonés:

Espejo? -- Ai toy

Eyaculación precoz? -- Ya tah

Insatisfación sexual? -- Komo ke yatah

Fin? -- Saka bo

Flaco? -- Yono komo

Ginecólogo? -- Yositoko tukuka

Homosexual? -- Tukuro taroto

Laxante? -- Saka lakaka

Panuelo? -- Kito mokito

Me robaron la moto? -- Yanoveo miyamaha

SPANISH IN JAPANESE

How to say Spanish words in Japanese:

Mirror? -- **Alli estoy**(There I am)

Premature ejeculation? -- **Ya esta** (That's it)

Sexual dissatisfaction? -- **Como que, "ya está**?"
(What you mean, "that's it?")

The End? -- **Se acabó** (It's all over)

Skinny? -- **Yono Komo** (I don't eat)

Gynecologist? -- **Si toco tu cuca** (Yes, I touch your
pussy)

Homosexual? -- **Tu culo está roto** (Your butthole is
broke)

Laxative? -- **Saca la caca** (take out the doo-doo)

Handkerchief? -- **Quito moquito** (I take out the snot)

My motorcycle was stolen? -- **Ya no veo mi yamaha**
(I don't see my Yamaha)

Y, hablando de Japoneses en Mexico::

¿Has oído el caso de ese fugitivo que secuestró un autobús de turistas japoneses?   La policía tiene 5.000 fotos suyas.

> Have you heard about the case of that fugitive who held hostage a busload of Japanese tourists?   The police have 5,000 pictures of him.

Sayings
Dichos

These are not jokes, exactly, but various sayings, puns, and one-liners common to Mexican culture. Many can be dropped casually for a chuckle, even though people have heard them before.

NAME GAMES

These aren't really jokes or dichos, but just cute taglines like "See you later, alligator" or "No way, Jose", based on names. The most commonly heard is ¿Entiendes, Mendez?, often said to stress a point, like, "You understand me, boy?"

¿Entiendes, Mendez?

¿O te lo explico, Fredrico?

Que gacho, Nacho.

Ay Teresa, como me interesa!

Voy solo Manolo

Ay Maria, que punteria!.

(This one is from a TV show tagline. I've gotten a few laughs by turning into Que putaria!)

Como Santa Elena, cada dia mas buena.

(You hear this one in response to ¿Como esta?)

Hola, Hola, Coca Cola

¿Que te pasa, calabasa?

LETTER GAMES

These are "licence plate" sound-alikes: just pronounce the Spanish letters correctly. Similar to English depictions like 10SNE1 for "Tennis, anyone?" It's fun to make them up yourself, but these are all fairly common.

TKT -- Very common: Tecate Beer

OBDC -- **Obedece** "Obey!" Often seen in jokes like "The only four letters men (or women) need to know."

OGT -- **Ojete**. Means "asshole" but also a miser, tightwad, mean-spirited jerk.

+COTAS -- A pet store: the plus sign makes it **MAScotas**.

FAR+CIA -- Similarly , **Farmacia**, a pharmacy chain.

LIQUI2 -- A cute liquor store name, the 2 making it **Liquidos.**

K PRICIOS -- Capricios, a caprice or frolic. In this case the name of a day care center.

TBCYTDG1BB -- Te **besé y te dejé un bebe**. A classic. "I kissed you and I left you a baby."

T B C, T U C, T D G, G G G -- Similar. **Te besé, te usé, te dejé, He he he**. I kissed you, I used you, I left you, ha, ha ha.

T N S L P P B N T S O -- Similar. **Tienes el pipi bien tieso.** . (You have a boner)

3R3S 1 1D10T4 -- This one works on sight, not sound, it doesn't take much imagination to see it saying **Eres una idiota.**

WATCHWORDS

These are little turns on words for comic effect, like saying "Infernal Revenue" or "The Excited States". Nice for spicing up conversation with a grin or two.

Burrocracia (Burocracia) -- Or **burrocrata**, a cute play on burocracia, stupidity of.

¿Es desastre? (¿Es de sastre?) -- A line for somebody who has a new suit. Play between "tailor made?" and "is it a disaster?"

Analfabestia (Analfabeta) -- Add an "s" to "illiterate" and it's more evocative, "beast" often meaning a brute or ignoramus.

Bodachera (boda) -- Mashup of wedding, and **borrachera**: a drunken bash.

Mula mable (Muy amble) Tossing "mule" into "you're so kind" or "thanks for being nice."

Mucho susto -- Funny alternative to **mucho gusto**, indicating scary.

¿Es de estaño? (de este año) -- Asked or said about someone's car or bling--"this year's model car" vs. "made out of tin."

De nalga (De nada) -- A cute, racier twist on "you're welcome" since **nalga** means "buttock".

Aguantala, güera -- Means "deal with it, blondie": sing to tune of "Guantanamera"

Caballo güero (Caballero) -- "Pale horse"... a gloss on "gentleman"--works best with gringos.

Defectuoso – "The defective" is a play on the use of **"DF" (de efe)** for the Federal District around Mexico City, where the **"Chilangos"** come from.

Dodge – An odd one, but Mexicans think that this word (prounced with long "o", or course) sounds like **dos.** So you can say "**Ando de Dodge. Dodge patas"** and get a chuckle. Especially if you make the two-fingered "walking" sign to reinforce the "two feet" thing. When they ask me in stores if I want a parking validation, I say, "**No, puro Dodge**" and they get it and grin.

Cancun? Con quién? – A nod and wink when somebody says they are going to Cancun on vacation. Kind of a "stays in Vegas" sort of arch knowing smirk.

Salud! Salió! – Somebody sneezes and you say **Salud**. They sneeze again and you say **Salio!** (it came out).

San Lunes – A semi-comic invocation of an unofficial "Holy Day"; Monday, when nobody goes to work because they are hung over from Sunday's drinking.

Es la ley – In a similar vein refers to social behavior so common as to be almost obligatory. A guy says he's going home and get drunk, or is going to cheat on his wife while she's visiting her mother and somebody says, "**Es la ley, verdad?**" Pretty much a guy thing.

Bodachera – A portmanteau of boda (wedding) and borrachera (a drunken bash). Self-explanatory.

Sana, sana, colita de rana – This is a refrain for little kids, but adults get a kick out of it. It means, "Get well, get well, frog's tail," but the idea is to get well, said in a cute manner.

Que llueva, que llueva, la vieja está en la cueva – The old lady being in the cave because of the rain is just a version of "It's raining, it's pouring…" and can be sung to the same tune for a bit of cutesy that generall draws a smile.

Lero, lero (Often with **candelero)** added. Sing-song delivery: is equivalent to "neener, neener" or "nyah, na, na, na, na" as a teasing rebuke.

Ay María qué puntería! – "Wow Maria, good aim!" A TV series with the comedy and film star "La India Maria" a personification of the indigeous in modern Mexican life.

No hay, no hay – This line, generally delivered with a helpless shrug, is from the old TV show by the amazing Héctor Suarez and is a good rejoinder as well as a sort of sociopolitical commentary.

Que nos pasa? – "What's happening to us" was the name of Suarez' show. The line is associated with a querulous old man's voice and can be used as a sort of "WTF".

Queremos rock! – Another Suarez personage, "El Destroyer" was always shouting "We want rock" and it can be a useful tagline even today.

> *Hector Suarez was a comedic genius. It's worth looking him up on Google, and see the delivery for some of these lines.*

Méndigo – when properly accented on the "i" means "beggar" or "mendicant". But when accented on the "e" like this is something entirely different, a chump or **pendejo.** Can also be an adjective, indicating that something sucks. One of the most famous applications is this sticker/T-shirt logo Which twists the famous **"Hecho en Mexico"** (Made in Mexico) symbol into "Made into a chump" or "Made a fool out of."

Wey, Buey, Guey – This polymorphus word is hard to nail down. **Buey** means an ox, steer, or other castrated animal, but the other forms can be anything from insults to just words like, "homes", "bro", "buddy", or "asshole" used generically.

This popular T-shirt is a nice bilingual pun that one-ups "I'm with stupid".

A variation:

FUNNY NAMES

Mexicans are pretty good at putting cute names on businesses, especially taco shops.

These can often be fairly subtle, and generally escape the notice of foreigners. For instance, most non-Mexicans would pass the **Comida China Loa** in Tijuana and see just a Chinese food place named Loa. But Mexicans laugh at the sign on sight because the Chinaloa is a pun on Sinaloa state.

A very famous taqueria in Guadalajara is Tacos Tumbras. The name means nothing... but when read as **Te acostumbras**, means something like "You get used to it." Doubly clever is **Taco Riendo** because it means "Laughing Taco" but "really" means **Esta corriendo**, "It's running".

Similar name-plays include **El Tacolgando** (It's hanging up), the cute **Tacos 9 Citos**, meaning **Tacos Nuevocitos** (brand new tacos) **Taco Mible** (**Esta Comible** – It's edible) **Tacorrible** (which should be obvious) **Tacos Tao** (a very subtle one whose logo of a guy in a sombrero dozing makes clear the **Esta Costa'o**, meaning "He's laying down"). Many love the **Taquero Mucho** which says **Te quiero mucho** (I love you a lot).

Needless to say, bars also take on some sly names. Like **Bar Celona, Bar Buda** which indicates not Buddhism, but **barbuda**... a bearded lady. And best of all the **Bar Ato**... **barato**, you can't get better than "cheap".

You hear funny names floating around, not real people but mythical personages like Jack Mehoff, Heywood Jablowmie and Mike Hunt. These include:

Elsa Pato -- El Zapato -- The shoe

Cindy Nero -- Sin Dinero -- Broke

Lola Mento -- Lo Lamento -- So sorry

Elvis Teck -- El Bistek -- Steak

Alex Cremento -- Al Excremento -- Al Shit

Elsa Nitario -- El Sanitario -- The Bathroom

Esteban Dido -- Este Bandido -- This robber

Eddy Ficio -- Edificio -- Building

Elvio Lado -- El Violado -- The raped guy

Aquiles Pinto Parededs -- Aqui Les Pinto Paredes -- Walls painted here

Hal Colico -- Alcolico -- Alcoholic

Alma Madero -- El Mamadero -- The sucker

Dolores Delano -- Dolores Del Ano -- Pain in the ass

Monica Galindo -- Moni Caga Lindo -- Moni shits pretty

EL COLMO

This form of joke is hard to translate, but not that hard to grasp when you see a couple. El colmo of something is the "height of it", "the last word" in it, the worst example, the absurd extreme.

¿Que es el colmo de camello?

Que lo estén jorobando.

The colmo of a camel is being a hunchback.

¿Cuál es el colmo de un enano?

Que lo pare un policía y le diga, ¡ALTO!

The colmo of a midget is a cop yelling "ALTO!" at him. (**Alto** meaning both "halt" and "tall")

¿Cuál es el colmo de un sordo?

Que al morir le dediquen un minuto de silencio.

The colmo of a deaf person is when he dies they dedicate a minute of silence to him.

¿Cuál es el colmo de un ciego?

Que le dé miedo la oscuridad.

The colmo of a blind man is fear of the dark.

¿Cuál es el colmo de un mudo?

Que lo arresten y le digan que tiene derecho a guardar silencio.

The colmo of a deaf man is getting arrested and told he has the right to keep silent.

¿Cuál es el colmo de un policia?

Tener dos esposas.

The colmo of a policeman is having two wives.
(Or, two pair of handcuffs, same word)

¿Cuál es el colmo de un Robot?

Tener nervios de acero.

The colmo of a robot is having nerves of steel.

¿Cuál es el colmo de un semáforo?

Decir: no me mires que me estoy cambiando

The colmo of a stoplight is saying, Don't look while I'm changing.

¿Cuál es el colmo de un ciego?

Enamorarse a primera vista.

The colmo of a blind person is falling in love at first sight.

¿Cuál es el colmo de un fantasma mafioso?

Que le diga a la policía: No me atrapará vivo.

The colmo of a mafioso ghost is telling the coppers, You'll never take me alive.

¿Cuál es el colmo de un diskette?

Tomar Viagra para ptcharconvertirse en disco duro.

The colmo of a diskette is taking Viagra to become a hard drive.

PRONUNCIATION NOTES

Sometimes correct pronunciation is more important in jokes and puns than in normal speech. This is a brief guide... you can pick up examples in movies, songs, and learning tapes.

As far as pronunciation, remember that ñ is pronounced like the "ny" in "canyon", ll is pronounced the same as y (either as in English or the Spain or "classy" way, in which ella is pronounced as "Asia"). An initial g or j is pronounced as "h" unless followed by a u, in which case the diphthong sounds as "wh." H is always silent. If a word ends in l or r it is accented on the last syllable. All other words are accented on the second to last syllable unless another syllable bears the accent mark. Vowels are simple, pure and always pronounced the same":

a--as in "ah" or "mama"

e--like the long "a" in "make" or "way"

i--like the long "e" in "feel" or "see"

o--as in "old" or "no"

u--without the initial "y" sound of English, as in "kudos" or "rude"

ABOUT THE AUTHOR
AND COVER ARTIST

"Cabo Bob" may be a **nombre de pluma** but he's an institution among travelers and expatriates in Mexico, where the original Mexican Slang 101 is a best-seller with over 100,000 copies of the little yellow paperback out there in the right hands. It's worth visiting. www.Slang101.com to see what he's up to...and don't miss the videos

We're delighted to have another cover illustration by Jessica Creager, who created the famous Cabo Bob character in the hammock for the cover of Mexican Slang 101.

Ms. Creagar is a noted Seattle artist with fans in many genres, in addition to her work as a patent attorney and skating as the demon jammer for the Rat City Rollers roller derby team.

BOOKS BY LINTON ROBINSON

Fans of these books, and of Mexico, will also like these books by Cabo Bob's alter ego, Linton Robinson

IMAGINARY LINES is a collection of essays about the border that go far beneath the usual portrait of Mexico and frontier culture.

MAYAN CALENDAR GIRLS is a wild, sexy romp across the whole Mayan end-of-the-world mythos... and some hot, tough, fun girls

SWEET SPOT is a bold, romantic, political adventure set in Mazatlan.

FOR YOUR DAMNED LOVE is a bold adventure that sprawls from Cabo to Vallarta to the Nayarit highlands.

COMING IN 2014 are several major new titles, including award-winning pieces in **TIJUANA NOCTURNES** and a major border novel, **MARY OF ANGELS.**

To take a look at these Mexico books, visit the author's page at:
www.amazon.com/author/LintonRobinson

181

BE A PART OF THIS BOOK

Be a partner with Cabo Bob... if you know some great jokes or "Mexicanismos" send them in. If we use them in a future edition, you get credited. Send to mexican@slang101.com or just click HERE.

GET NEW EDITIONS

If you want to get new editions of Mexican Humor 201, if we add new material, just sign up and we'll mail you the new copies when the come out. slang101.com/mail (Updates) Or click HERE.

Made in the USA
Middletown, DE
12 September 2018